GRITS 'N GREENS
AND MISSISSIPPI THINGS

Grits 'n Greens

Published and Marketed by
Parlance Publishing
P.O. Box 841
Columbus, Mississippi 39703

First Edition
1st Printing

Printed in the
United States of America

ISBN 0-9721032-0-1

Library of Congress Control Number
2002090502

Designed by: Jackie Taylor, Greenwood Springs, MS.
Cover Photography by: Chris Jenkins, Columbus, MS.

On the cover: "Mother Goose"
a.k.a. Edwina Williams, a children's storyteller,
and Thomas Brevard Howard,
both of Columbus, Mississippi.
Cover Location: The Griffin Home (1896), a
Victorian Bed & Breakfast in Columbus.

CONTENTS

PREFACE

I have been thinking about this book for more years than I care to remember, throughout which time I've been collecting research material and writing about Mississippi for other publications. Most writers are pack-rats. We save everything, because just as surely as we dispose of something one day, the next day, a big story will come along and we'll need the exact piece of information that we no longer have. So rather than agonize over purging my burgeoning files, I decided to put them to use and finally write a book about my Mississippi and feature people, places, food, and stories that make our state unique.

As I drafted this book, I wondered what category it would fit into. It is not exactly a travel guide, not entirely a cookbook, not a lengthy and precise historical account, not fiction, not high drama, not comedy, and not a literary masterpiece. What it is, I believe, is a nice little book that tells a few interesting facts about the state's regions, and in the process, emphasizes the things that Mississippians love most: good food, good times, and good stories. Perhaps true, died-in-the-wool, native Mississippians will see that it's an attempt to honor those who came before us, whose hard work and talents helped to form the state we know and love today. And it's a way to keep in touch with what's near and dear to us now. So there is no category that this book will fit into. It is just a little book about grits and greens and Mississippi things.

So many people made "Grits and Greens" possible, and I am grateful. Thanks so much to those who spoke with me, shared stories and recipes, sent me new and updated information, and smiled when they heard the title. Thanks, especially, to those who cared enough about Mississippi's history and happenstance to support my effort to publish a book that covers the state.

Many who saw the book in draft form said, "What a good idea! I want to send one to...(kids, friends, relatives) because they will love to read positive things about Mississippi." There are so many good things happening here in the Magnolia State, and so often, friends and relatives who live elsewhere seldom hear about anything but a sensationalized account of a bizarre event.

It is my hope that you will be encouraged to take a road trip around the state and see what you've been missing!

Sylvia Higginbotham
Columbus, Mississippi

INTRODUCTION

I read a review of Southern fiction that asked, "Is the South still Southern?" My immediate response was, "Not like it used to be." But then, I thought, Mississippi is still the most Southern of all the southern United States, so perhaps the reviewer has not ventured into the mighty Magnolia State. Before he writes about us, he would do well to pay us a visit, for being here is much different than writing from a distance.

What Mississippi "used to be" to me was playing in the woods behind our house, where a cool, clear spring provided drinks of water on a hot summer day. Neighborhood kids, what few there were, used fertile imaginations to conjure up images of early Indians whose "mounds" and arrowheads were sometimes found. And as the kids got older, at certain times of the year, "rabbit tobacco" was ready to be harvested and rolled in old newspapers, when the courage could be mustered to sneak a naughty smoke.

Mississippi used to be Sunday at church and the occasional dinner on the ground, with the women of the church preparing and serving their special recipes. And Mississippi used to be swimming in the summer at Lake Waukaway near the old Stafford Springs Resort --between Meridian and Laurel-- where the clean, natural spring water was so cold even the chubbiest of children turned an odd shade of purple.

That's the way it was in South Mississippi, anyway. Every region has its own set of circumstances and memories, and for many Mississippians, those distant memories are forever embellished as the best of times. Throughout this book we'll look at the regions, and try to point out the people and places that contribute to each region's uniqueness.

And here's an example of the people who make the region unique: For the many people who think that Southern ladies of a certain age wilt in the sun, we're pleased to call attention to such spectacular women as the late Miss Georgia Young Hopkins (1890-1985), a lifelong resident of Columbus, as were her parents and grandparents. "Miss Georgia," as she was called until her death at 95, was a spinster, of sorts, but not the white glove kind who never saw direct sunlight. Rather, Miss Georgia was a lady who loved to work the soil. She had an old mule which she hitched up to plow her garden spot, and from that spot, Miss Georgia grew legendary flowers and vegetables. People in Columbus still talk about her wonderful asparagus and the special sauce she served with it. She was not only a gardener extraordinaire, but a renowned cook, as well. She was a lady with a sunny disposition and a great sense of humor, which meant that Miss Georgia was in demand at parties and social functions.

The local history room at the Columbus Public Library has a file on the Hopkins family, and a big box of Miss Geogria's recipes, some of which you'll find in this book. In the box is an old ledger filled with hand-written recipes, and completely indexed by recipe and name of the person who claimed it. Sometimes, an indexed recipe entry would have three or four names, with each recipe slightly varied. She wanted to give each person credit. So many ladies like Miss Georgia give Mississippi its special flavor.

The Delta is perhaps the most unique place in the state. Someone once said that the Mississippi Delta is the most Southern place on Earth. I believe that to be true, but I also believe that indeed, our "Southern-ness" is slowly slipping away. Except in rare, isolated pockets of the state, our speech is becoming an homogenous blend of midwestern and New South, thanks to television, movies, and the amalgamated patois that our children hear at school. The soft, genteel way of speaking employed by our grandmothers and maiden aunts is seldom heard today. But it lives on in our memories, and that's one of the wonderful things about being Southern. We seem to have the ability to retain the best of the old -- perhaps even to romanticize it-- and somehow find a place for it in the way we live today.

Our lifestyles are not as agrarian, for we've left the farms to work in offices and industry. Rather than growing peas, beans, corn and tomatoes in fields and backyard gardens, we join our urban neighbors at the local supermarket, scouring the produce aisles for the freshest home-grown vegetables. In fact, we cherish anything home-made or hand-made. Could it be that we do truly miss the Mississippi of our memories?

We build new houses and fill them with antiques and old things; we buy rocking chairs and front porch swings and we use them at every opportunity; we watch TV re-runs of Andy Griffith of Mayberry, and we fondly recall "the good old days." So often, our kids grow up, get educated, and move away, yet many still yearn to come back home.

It's no wonder. Life is pretty good here. We grew up hearing about the state's attributes from the plethora of Mississippi-born writers, among them William Faulkner, Eudora Welty, Tennessee Williams, Willie Morris, James Street, and so many more. They helped to convince us that indeed, our Mississippi is a special place.

Mississippi is chock full of wonderful, unique nuances --with grits and greens only two of thousands-- but there's a story about this down-home fare. I heard the term "grits 'n' greens" when I was a very young bride living in Brooklyn, New York, with my Navy-man husband whose ship was dry-docked at the Brooklyn Navy Base. On a picnic at Prospect Park, we heard a familiar accent, and knew the South-speaking woman must be from home. As it happened, she was a fellow Mississippian who said she'd do most anything for a home-cooked meal that included fried chicken, cheese grits, turnip greens, blackberry cobbler, and sweet tea. But she way she said 'grits 'n greens' stayed with me. I loved the way it sounded, becaue it sounded like home. Since that time, I've associated "grits and greens" with the Mississippi of my mind, so naturally, it's the title for this book.

As with any Southern writer or storyteller, there's always something more to add, and this addition is about the artist whose art represents the diversity of the Magnolia State. You'll see her sketches throughout the book. Her name is Sharon

Grant Roan, known to her friends as Sherrie.

Sherrie and I are not related, but we share Aunt Daisy, actually Sherrie's aunt and my friend. For years, whenever I saw Aunt Daisy in her hometown of Laurel, she told me about her niece Sherrie who also lived in Columbus, and that Sherrie was an artist. Our paths never crossed because Sherrie was involved with a fine arts group and my artistic activities were in the performing arts. Once, her work caught my attention while it was on exhibit at the local library, though I didn't know that the fine artist who painted the gray-haired lady wearing a hat with a cat--who looked so familiar to me-- was Aunt Daisy's neice Sherrie, for I'd never heard Sherrie's last name.

On a fall Sunday afternoon in 1999, Aunt Daisy called me to say that she was in Columbus to visit Sherrie, and could I come over? As I walked into Sherrie's den, the first thing I saw was the oil painting of the familiar-looking gray-haired lady.

"You bought the painting I wanted!"-- I exclaimed. Sherrie looked somewhat surprised, and said, "No, I painted it." The painting of the lady whose familiarity had haunted me for years was none other than someone I had seen as a young child, "Miss Nanny" Ritchie, who was Sherrie's great aunt. For a few years, the Ritchie family had also lived in eastern Jones County, not too far from our place. So my association with the artist Sharon Roan began, indirectly, a long time ago, and unbeknownst to either of us, our parents were friends back then.

Thanks to all who supplied the recipes found throughout this book, which are used in conjunction with some from my mother's collection of old cook books, some from Miss Georgia's collection, and others from old newspapers and tattered magazines. I make no claim to being a great cook myself, but I come from a long line of wonderful cooks and I do love good food. Many of the recipes are what I call "old Southern." In this book, you won't find the new gourmet creations they're teaching at the Culinary Arts Institute at Mississippi University for Women. Some of the young chefs coming out of the culinary program are so talented they scare me. But then, they can write their own book about the new cuisine, and I'll buy one and add it to my collection of old-fashioned, down-home cookbooks.

When Blanche DuBois, a fictional, fading Mississippi belle, said in *A Streetcar Named Desire*, "I've always depended on the kindness of strangers," she summed up the way down-home folk feel about food and friendships: there's always room for more. That's the Mississippi way.

Sharon Roan's painting of "Miss Nanny."

Chapter 1
History and Happenstance

Mississippi is a gentle land of myth and majesty to those of us who know and love it. And those who don't, well, they've made their opinions known. For the most part, there's a tranquility about the state. Quiet evenings when the sun is setting on a Delta cotton field --or an early morning on the misty Pascagoula River, waiting for a big blue gill to bite--these are the tranquil times that feed our souls. These are the times I'm most proud to be a Mississippian. For a gypsy at heart to profess being proud to be anyplace that demands putting down roots is indeed a feat. For some reason, Mississippi attracts gypsies and vagabonds. Did you know that the king and queen of the gypsies in America are interred at Rose Hill Cemetery in Meridian? Since 1915, the gravesites of the Gypsy Royal Family have been recipients of unusual gifts, among them fruits and fruit juices left by people from far and near.

Long before the arrival of the gypsies, another vagabond of sorts made his way here from Spain. Hernando DeSoto and his band of Spaniards trekked across what is now Mississippi in or around 1540. From all accounts, while searching for gold, DeSoto found civilization in the midst of the new country; one that may have been older than his own. It appears that he traded with two of the big three Indian nations in residence here at that time --the Choctaw and the Chickasaw. The Chickasaws were more aggressive; they took issue with the Spaniards' habit of looting their villages and taking their people to serve as "burden bearers." By the time DeSoto reached the Mississippi River, it looks as though he had worn out his welcome with the Chickasaw, for there had been skirmishes along the way.

The Natchez nation inhabited the land to the south of here, along with the Biloxi and Pascagoula tribes. The Yazoo, the Ofo, and the Tunica were in the western region. Nanih Waiya, the mythical mother-mound that gave birth to the big Choctaw nation, is near Philadelphia. The second largest nation, the Natchez, was ruled by the Great Sun. The sun-worshipping Natchez --dwellers of the Grand Village of the Great Sun-- had an advanced civilization. They also believed that their chief was the child of the sun.

After the French came into South Mississippi in 1699, wars between the French and the Natchez finally destroyed the Natchez nation. The Choctaws and their cousins the Chickasaws held their own with the Europeans who came to settle the new world, though most of the native Americans were eventually banished to the Indian Territory, now Oklahoma.

Traces of Mississippi's first citizens remain with us today. Apart from the Choctaw settlement in Neshoba County, about 20 counties in the state have Indian names, and even more cities. Among the counties are Amite, Coahoma, Issaquena, Noxubee, Tallahatchie, Yazoo, while the cities include Biloxi, Buckatunna, Escatawpa, Itta Bena, Noxapater, Pachuta, Shubuta, Toomsuba, and Winona, among others.

Mississippi became a state in 1817. The whites, who came in search of fertile soil and their own land, prospered if they settled near rivers or roads. Cotton production was responsible for the plantations that sprang up along the Mississippi River and the Tombigee River. Natchez was so prosperous from cotton money, it became one of the richest towns in the country, with more millionaires than any place other than New York City, according to reports of the day.

Grand homes were built, with furnishings and materials shipped over from Europe. Indeed, Natchez was considered a city of the world, an aristocratic society where the per capita wealth was more then $4500, while the national average was less than $700. Natchez was also considered very cosmopolitan, with Pride of China trees lining the streets, two hospitals, a theatrical group, a race track, and of course the notorious "Natchez Under the Hill" activities of gambling and river boat traffic.

South Mississippi's Piney Woods farmers didn't build plantations. These fiercely independent folk apparently had little interest in acquiring or showing wealth. Lumbermen and railroads changed things in the 1850s, and then the Civil War wreaked havoc on the economy and the way of life for most Mississippians. Also in South Mississippi, the Gulf Coast area was developing its resort potential, where planters and others of wealth spent their summers in the refreshing breeze from the Gulf.

When war became inevitable and the South chose to secede from the Union, Mississippi was the second state to secede, on January 9, 1861. U.S. Senator Jefferson Davis became the first and only president of the newly formed Confederate States of America. Not all regions of the state shared Davis's conviction, however. Jones County was poor and just getting settled in 1860. There were few slaveholders, and the constituency requested that their delegate to the secession convention in Jackson oppose secession. After it was learned that their delegate sided with the secessionists, the Jones Countians hanged him in effigy.

Most of the men fought for the Confederacy because they were honorable, though one Newt Knight held out. When he was finally drafted, the quiet man refused to fight and was made a hospital orderly. He soon convinced himself that it was a rich man's war and a poor man's fight, and when he heard that the farms and homes in his beloved Jones County were being looted, he and a few other soldiers went home to stay. Knight and his friends formed a company of their own and refused to return to the war, thus they were labeled "deserters."

One story says that when the Confederate cavalry --aided by bloodhounds-- tried to find the men they considered deserters, the wives of the deserters choked the dogs with meat sprinkled with red pepper. Some of the deserters were caught and hanged, and the area where the hanging occurred is still referred to as "Cracker's Neck."

Newt Knight and his band of men attracted the attention of the press, and were reported to have had their county, Jones, secede from Mississippi after the state seceded from the Union. No documentation of such a move has been found, though the rumors persisted and were memorialized in Mississippi native James Street's novel,

Tap Roots. Knight and his men soon fell from grace, and once the war was over, loyal Confederates in the county voted to change the name from Jones (for John Paul Jones) to Davis (for Jefferson Davis), though the original name was reestablished during Reconstruction.

Passions ran high during the Civil War. It has been said that a Catholic Bishop in Natchez was chastised and temporarily relieved of his duties because he refused to pray for President Abraham Lincoln. Perhaps he was related to or knew some of the 80,000 or so Mississippi men who served in the Confederate States of America army. Some never returned; many who did were either maimed or mentally drained. About 600 historic markers throughout the state connect the past to the present and make us mindful of the fact that terror and turmoil once lived in our own Magnolia State.

After the war, the South was in economic ruin, and the rebuilding of this once proud region was slow and arduous. After the bloody War Between the States ended in 1865, the soldiers who survived returned to a "New South" that was alien to the old. Civil government was restored, and Congress voted Mississippi back into the Union in 1870. The overthrow of carpetbag rule was a gradual process.

Black Mississippians, too, had major adjustments to make in forging a new way of life and a place for themselves amid the changes. Some ambitious former slaves from Jefferson Davis' brother's plantation created their own town in the heart of the Mississippi Delta. Mound Bayou is the oldest all-black municipality in the United States. It was founded in 1887 and incorporated in 1898. The people wanted a place "where God and liberty dwelt." Land could be purchased for $8 per acre at that time, and it was soon learned that owning land established a strong sense of pride among the people. Mound Bayou is still basically an all-black community, and like many other places in the country, it is looking for ways to encourage economic development.

By the late 1800s, the days of grace and grandeur were gone. Even the era in which grandeur once flourished seem mythical, as if in a far and forgotten memory. But Mississippians are stalwart people who know how to endure. We know that most hardships are short-lived, and we firmly believe that when hard times come, "This, too, shall pass." And so it did.

Mississippians also called upon their inherent mettle to withstand World War I, the Great Depression, World War II, Korea, Viet Nam, and now parts of the Middle East. Between the Korean Cold War and the Viet Nam Conflict, integration occurred, which created still more changes and adjustments for blacks and whites in the Magnolia State.

But throughout the turbulent years of wars and political and social unrest, the state still spawned Nobel Prize-winning writers, award winning actors and musicians, nationally recognized artists, teachers, medical researchers, aviators, inventors, and through it all, we acquired a serious list of **Mississippi "firsts."**

- The first State Bar Association in the U.S. was organized in Natchez in 1821.
- In 1839, the Mississippi Legislature passed one of the first laws in the English speaking world that protected the rights of married women.
- The first state-supported college for women was founded in Columbus in 1884.
- Coca-Cola was first bottled by Joseph Beidenharn in Vicksburg in 1894.
- The Neshoba County Fair, started in 1889, is the nation's oldest campground fair.
- The first 4-H Club in the country began in Holmes County in 1907.
- The first Parents Teachers Assoc. (PTA) was founded in Crystal Springs in 1909.
- Quinine was first used as a treatment for malaria in Bolivar County in 1916.
- The world's first round trip transoceanic flight was performed in 1928 by H.T. Merrill of Iuka. The flight to England was in a plane loaded with ping-pong balls.
- The official world's record for keeping a plane aloft is held by Al and Fred Key of Meridian. They re-fueled in the air and kept their plane aloft for 653 hours and 34 minutes in 1935.
- The National Association of Junior Auxiliaries began in Greenville in 1941.
- Mississippi is the first state in the nation to have a planned system of junior colleges.
- The nation's oldest land grant college for African-Americans is Alcorn State University near Port Gibson.
- The first black woman to become a celebrated diva with the Metropolitan Opera was Leontyne Price, a native of Laurel.
- The world's first kidney autotransplant was performed at University Medical Center in Jackson in 1962.
- The world's first human lung transplant was also performed at UMC, in 1963.
- The world's most widely-used physiology textbook for physicians was published by Dr. Arthur C. Guyton, a native of Oxford.
- The world's largest collection of blues music is in the Blues Archives at Ole Miss.
- MTV (Music Television Video) was founded in 1981 by native Mississippian Bob Pittman when he was 32. Pittman hails from Brookhaven.
- Mississippi was the first state to adopt a homestead exemption law.
- The first African-American woman to host a major multi-network television talk show was Oprah Winfrey, a native of Kosciusko.
- The largest United States Department of Agriculture (USDA) research facility is in the little Mississippi Delta town of Stoneville, near Leland. This massive, impressive research center has been called the Silicon Valley of Agriculture. Many agricultural researchers from Mississippi State University operate out of the Stoneville facility.
- Locals say that Greenville boasts more writers per capita than any other town in the country. The Greenville Writers Exhibit at the local library features William Alexander Percy, Shelby Foote, Ellen Douglas, Walker Percy, Hodding Carter, David Cohn, Beverly Lowry, Bern Keating, and more.
- The Norris Bookbinding Company of Greenwood is the largest Bible re-binding plant in the nation.
- More than 75 percent of the world's supply of farm-raised catfish comes from Mississippi.

Chapter 2
The River Cities and Mississippi's Rivers

From its auspicious beginnings at Lake Itasca, Minnesota, where a marker standing near a shallow outlet reads: "Here 1,475 feet above the ocean the mighty Mississippi River begins to flow on its winding way 2,552 miles to the Gulf of Mexico." This mighty river has made history in its wake; it has created the history of a country. Since human habitation began, the river has provided food, transportation, and commerce. Today the river represents all the above, as well as outstanding scenery in the dense forests, towering bluffs, and flat delta lands that border the murky waters.

Legendary places of history and romance line the south Mississippi leg of the river --Natchez, Vicksburg, Greenville-- all of whom still hear the calliope music as the riverboats round the bend. Though Greenville is definitely a river city, it is more closely associated with the Delta, therefore the overview of Greenville is in the Delta chapter.

Natchez

There's a dichotomy in the lovely Natchez unlike any other place in the country, perhaps the world. Natchez is older than New Orleans by two years, and today it is truly the grande dame of the South. The quiet grandeur that soothes the soul has dibs on my heart, but then, there's the intrigue associated with Natchez Under the Hill. In its heyday, it was a walk on the wild side for the prim and proper Natchezians on top of the hill.

Natchez Under the Hill is still a big draw in this river city, just as it was in the early days. It's where the riverboats landed and deposited the gamblers and others who made Under the Hill a "red light district." Saloons were frequented by gamblers, rowdy frontiersmen, and ladies of the evening. One evangelist of the day called it "...the worst hell-hole on earth," while others called it the "Barbary Coast of Mississippi." The place was surely a source of controversy!

Riverboats --the Delta Queen and the Mississippi Queen-- still dock Under the Hill. Today, it's a place of good restaurants, shops, and a great river view. Perhaps still reminiscent of the olden days, a permanently-docked riverboat-type casino is nearby.

It's easy to see that Natchez was once home to more millionaires than any place else in the United States, with the exception of New York City. Many of the homes built by the millionaires are available for touring during the annual Spring and Fall Pilgrimage. See more about "Pilgrimages" in the Mississippiana section.

Longwood, Natchez

Natchez has the largest number of pre-Civil War structures in the United States, many of which have been restored to perfection. The architectural details of the homes are truly amazing. At least one or two interesting stories surround each of the homes --from past liaisons involving historical figures-- to the "Goat Castle" murders. It's all part of the mystique that sets Natchez apart.

There's concrete evidence of one famous Natchez story that involves the still unfinished Longwood. The magnificent dome-topped mansion is the largest remaining octagonal house in the country and it remains a superb example of the mid-19th century Moorish style. Prominent architect Samuel Sloan of Philadelphia designed Longwood to be the 32-room showplace for the enormously wealthy Dr. Haller Nutt and his family, though interior work on Longwood ceased when the Civil War erupted and the Pennsylvania construction crew returned home. Before the craftsmen left, they completed the massive exterior with its white Moorish columns and arches which fronted all eight sides of the red brick house. The Byzantine dome still today evokes awe. The home featured a very advanced lighting and ventilation system.

Dr. Nutt was a cotton planter who had vast holdings in Mississippi and Louisiana. He was also a Yankee sympathizer, though his affinity for the Union did not prevent federal troops from burning his cotton fields, which were said to be valued at more than $3 million. Dr. Nutt was morally and financially devastated. According to legend, Dr. Nutt fled to Vicksburg to seek intervention from Union General U.S. Grant, but he encountered bad weather, contracted pneumonia, and died. His family continued to live on at Longwood, in the basement that they shared briefly with the husband and father. Members of the Nutt family continued to live in the cool, rambling, multi-room basement until 1968.

Today, this amazing reminder of "the South that was" is owned and maintained by the Pilgrimage Garden Club. It is open daily, and it is a National Historic Landmark, one of the many in Natchez.

There's a true story told in Natchez about Ibrahima, an African prince who was captured by a warring tribe in Africa and sold into slavery. Around 1788, he arrived in Natchez and was bought by a local planter. About 20 years later, he was recognized by the planter's friend, Dr. John Cox, whose life had been saved in Africa by Ibrahima's father. Dr. Cox wanted Ibrahima to be returned to Africa, where he would be a king. Finally, the planter freed the slave in 1820, and a newspaper helped to raise the money for Ibrahima's return to Africa. According to legend, the former slave made it as far as the African coast, but died before reaching the place of his birth. Learn more about black history in America at the Africa House and the William Johnson House, both in Natchez.

About 30 miles south of Natchez on Highway 61, the town of **Woodville** is one of those old front porch places that novelists love. The state's oldest church is here, Woodville Baptist, built in 1803, and so is Rosemont, the boyhood home of the President of the Confederacy, Jefferson Davis. The house was built around 1810. Before Davis became the CSA president, he served the country well as a graduate of the U.S. Military Academy at West Point, a U.S. Army officer for eight years, a U.S. Congressmen, two terms as a U.S. Senator, and he served as U.S. Secreatry of War from 1853 until 1857. Jefferson Finis Davis was indeed an American patriot.

Six miles north of Natchez on Highway 61 is the remarkable old town of Washington, home of the historic Jefferson College. In the 1800s, it was the seat of culture for the region, and the center of political activity.

Jefferson College, which began classes in 1802, was the first institution for higher education in the Old Southwest. Among the people associated with it were Jefferson Davis, a student; John James Audubon, an art teacher, and Aaron Burr, a prominent political figure who was arraigned for treason here. Classes were held at Jefferson College until the 1960s, when the buildings were restored to the 1800s and the campus became a museum.

Not too far north of Natchez find the pretty town of **Port Gibson**, the town that Union General Ulysses S. Grant said was "...too beautiful to burn." It is the home of Grand Gulf Military Monument Park, and near Port Gibson stands the hallowed and haunting Ruins of Windsor, the last vestiges of a grand plantation. The cost of Windsor's construction was $175,000, a princely sum in the late 1850s, when some families were lucky to have a hundred dollars a year. The magnificent mansion was left unscathed by the Union army during the Civil War, but was burned to the ground at the hands of a careless smoker in 1890. Twenty-three giant columns --the Ruins-- are all that's left of what was once the largest mansion ever built in Mississippi. The ruins have been seen in many movies, including "Raintree County," starring Elizabeth Taylor and Montgomery Clift. Also in Port Gibson is the Mississippi Cultural Crossroads, a place to showcase the talents of local quilters, some of whom can be seen quilting most days.

Natchez and the surrounding towns take pride in entertaining at long and leisurely dinner parties, and they may be as formal and festive as the hostess desires, or they may be casual and comfortable. On occasion, the party may be started with an old favorite "Planter's Punch" recipe that originated in Jamaica, but made its way to plantations along the River Road. The lemonade recipe is for those who don't imbibe in spirits but appreciate refreshment.

The recipes that follow are among the things you're likely to be served at a dinner party in Natchez, according to those who live there.

PLANTER'S PUNCH

1/4 cup fresh lime juice
3 tabsp. sugar
2 teasp. grenadine syrup
1/2 teasp. Agnostura bitters
1/4 cup dark rum (optional)
4 cups fresh orange juice
4 cups crushed ice
Garnish with cherries

Stir the lime juice, sugar, grenadine, and bitters in a two quart pitcher until the sugar dissolves. Pour in rum and orange juice; fill glasses with crushed ice. Place garnish on stirrers. Serves 6.

AUNT LILY JUNE'S LEMONADE

1-1/2 cups sugar
3 cups ice water
8 large lemons, squeezed
1/2 cup fresh mint leaves
Ice cubes
1 tabsp. grated lemon zest

Bring to boil sugar and 2 of the 3 cups of water; stir until sugar dissolves. Boil for about five minutes, then stir in lemon juice, zest, and mint leaves if you use mint. Remove from heat, cover, and set aside for 30 minutes to cool before straining into pitcher; add remaining cup of water. Cover 2-quart pitcher with plastic wrap and chill. To serve, add a few ice cubes to the pitcher, along with fresh mint leaves or thin slice of lemon. Pour into ice-filled glasses. Serves 6.

OYSTER BISQUE

1 pint oysters
3 tabsp. butter
3 tabsp. flour
1 can mushroom soup
Melba rounds or party crackers
1/2 cup onions, minced
1 teasp. salt; pepper to taste
2 egg yolks, beaten
1 cup crackers, crushed

Boil oysters in their liquid; cool. When cooled, cut oysters in pieces. Melt butter, stir in flour, add mushroom soup. Add the oysters and oyster liquid, then onion, salt and pepper to taste; red pepper if you like. Add egg yolks and crushed crackers. Cook slowly for about ten minutes. Serve in a chafing dish with Melba rounds or party crackers.

MARINATED SHRIMP

Boil two pounds medium/large shrimp. Add salt and pepper to water. Cool shrimp; peel. Place the following ingredients in a quart jar:

1 cup vegetable oil
1/4 cup olive oil
1 lemon, thin sliced
Pimento strips
1/8 teasp. red pepper, 1/2 teasp. salt
1/2 teasp. Worcestershire sauce
2 large onions, thin sliced, in rings
1/2 teasp. garlic powder
4 green onions & tops, chopped

Except for shrimp, place all other ingredients in jar; mix well. Put shrimp in large bowl, then pour mixture from jar over shrimp. Cover; stir occasionally. Refrigerate 24 hours; serve on lettuce beds with pimento, onion slices, lemon slices and shrimp. Double for a crowd. This is superb because it can be made two days in advance.

CREOLA'S CURRY DIP

1 cup mayonnaise
1 teasp. grated ginger
1 clove garlic
1/2 teasp. salt
2 tabsp. chopped green onion
Curry powder, 1 teasp. minimum
Lemon juice to taste
Red pepper to taste

Use blender to blend all ingredients, except lemon juice. Blend thoroughly, then add lemon juice to taste. Serve surrounded by a variety of uncooked, fresh vegetables.

STUFFED EYE OF ROUND ROAST

2-1/2 lb. eye of round roast
1 cup lean ham, chopped
3 hard-boiled eggs, chopped
6 cloves garlic
1 tabsp. olive oil
Pepper, to rub
6 oz. can tomato paste
2 white onions, chopped
1 green pepper, chopped
1 tabsp. Worcestershire sauce
3 bay leaves
1 teasp. ground cumin

Use a long, sharp knife to cut a pocket, lengthwise, in the roast. Cut near the edges, but be careful not to cut through. Mix the ham and eggs and stuff into the cavity. Season roast with pepper, then rub with garlic cut in half. Insert the garlic into roast at intervals. Place large skillet over medium-high heat, heat olive oil, then brown roast on all sides. Add the tomato paste, onions, green pepper, Worcestershire, cumin and bay leaves. Cover and cook over low heat for 45 minutes per pound. Cut in half- inch slices; serves 6.

SOUTHERN PECAN CHICKEN

8 chicken breast halves
1 cup buttermilk
1 egg, beaten lightly
1 cup flour
1 cup pecans, ground
1/2 cup butter, melted
1/4 cup sesame seeds
1 tabsp. paprika
2 teasp. salt
Pepper to taste

Mix buttermilk and egg, place in shallow dish. In medium bowl, combine flour, ground pecans, sesame seeds, paprika, salt and pepper. First, dip chicken in buttermilk mixture and then in flour mixture. Place chicken in roasting pan, skin side up. Drizzle melted butter evenly over chicken. Bake at 350 degrees for about one hour, or until chicken is golden brown. Serves 8.

SARAH'S SEAFOOD CASSEROLE

1/2 cup chopped onion
1/2 cup chopped green pepper
1/2 cup chopped celery
1/2 cup margarine
2 cups milk
6 oz. crab meat
12 oz. shrimp
1/4 teasp. paprika
Red pepper to taste
1 can cream of shrimp soup
2/3 cup flour
1/2 teasp. minced garlic
1/2 teasp. salt

Saute` first three ingredients in margarine. Stir in flour; cook one minute. Add seasonings. Stir in soup and milk and cook until thickened. Layer crab and shrimp in casserole. Top with sauce (soup and other ingredients) and bake at 350 degrees for 30 minutes. Serves 6.

CARROTS IN CREAM SAUCE

2 lbs. carrots, thinly sliced
1 tabsp. butter
2 teasp. sugar
1/2 teasp. salt
1 tabsp. flour
1 cup cream (Half & Half)
Salt and pepper to taste
2 tabsp. minced parsley

Combine first four ingredients in large saucepan. Add two cups water; heat on high until it boils, then reduce heat and simmer for about 20 minutes, or until carrots are tender. Remove carrots from liquid, then bring liquid to boil and reduce to shiny glaze. Whisk flour into glaze, then cream. Continue whisking until mixture comes to a boil. Add salt and pepper to taste, reduce heat and simmer for about three minutes. Return carrots to sauce; heat through. Serves 8.

GOLDEN BROCCOLI

2 pkgs. frozen broccoli
Salt and pepper to taste
2 tabsp. lemon juice
1 can cream of chicken soup
1/2 cup Cheddar cheese

Follow package directions to cook broccoli in salted water until tender. Drain. Place broccoli in shallow serving dish. Sprinkle with lemon juice and pepper. Cover with soup, to which salt and pepper have been added. Sprinkle cheese on top, then place under broiler until cheese is melted and bubbly. Serves 8.

CAJUN CORN

4 large ears corn on the cob
1/2 cup milk
2 slices bacon, diced
1 cup chopped onion
1/2 cup chopped bell pepper
2 cups chopped tomatoes
1/2 teasp. dried thyme
1/2 teasp. salt
Black pepper to taste
Red pepper to taste

Cut corn off cob; should be about 3 cups. Break the cobs into pieces, add milk, then place in a saucepan. Cover, bring to a boil, then simmer for 10 minutes before discarding cobs. Cook bacon for 5 minutes or until crisp, then place on paper towel to drain. Save one tablespoon of bacon fat, to which the onion and bell pepper is added; cook until soft. Add the corn, tomatoes, thyme, salt and pepper, and simmer gently for about 10 minutes. Serves 4.

Since Natchez is connected to New Orleans by the Mississippi River, they are fairly close in distance and style, so it is not uncommon to see desserts associated with New Orleans served in Natchez. Remember that New Orleans cuisine is more Creole, which is city food, as compared to the country food of South Louisiana, which we know as very good, old-fashioned Cajun cookin', Cher! We'll see more of that later, but for now, here are a few desserts with a distinctly New Orleans flavor.

FRESH FRUIT VERMOUTH

Fresh figs, whole
Mandarin oranges
Peaches, halved
Sweet vermouth
Whipped cream, no sugar
Nutmeg, fresh and grated

Place fruit in bowl, then half-cover the fruit with vermouth. Marinate for about three hours, gently turning twice while marinating. Cover fruit entirely with whipped cream, turning over once to blend the vermouth and cream. Refrigerate for an hour, then serve with grated nutmeg on top.

NEW ORLEANS CHOCOLATE PIE

1 cup sugar
Scant 3 tabsp. cocoa
2-1/2 tabsp. flour
Pinch of salt
1/4 cup of butter
2 egg yolks, beaten
2 cups milk
1-1/2 teasp. vanilla
1 pie crust, baked (10 inch)
Meringue

Combine the sugar, cocoa, flour and salt in a large saucepan. Add the butter, egg yolks, and milk; cook the mixture over low heat until it is thick. Stir in the vanilla, pour the filling into the pie crust, cover with meringue and bake at 350 degrees for about 12 minutes, Cool before serving. Serves 8 generously.

BANANAS FOSTER

4 tabsp. butter
1/4 cup brown sugar, packed
1/2 teasp. ground cinnamon
2 tabsp. banana liqueur
4 med. bananas, halved lengthwise and crosswise
1/4 cup rum
4 scoops vanilla ice cream

In flambe` pan or skillet, melt butter. Add next three ingredients, stir to mix. Bring to a boil and simmer two minutes, then place bananas in sauce. Cook, stirring often, until bananas are soft, about four minutes. Serve over vanilla ice cream. Serves 4.

PLANTATION PIE

1/3 cup semi-sweet chocolate chips
2/3 cup granulated sugar
1/2 cup water
1/4 cup butter or margarine
1-1/2 teasp. vanilla extract

Batter:
1 cup all-purpose flour, sifted
3/4 cup sugar
1 teasp. baking powder
1/2 teasp. salt
1/2 cup milk
1/4 cup shortening
1/2 teasp. vanilla extract
1 egg
1 frozen pie shell, deep dish
6 ounces pecan pieces

Melt chocolate with water over low heat; add sugar. Stir constantly until mixture begins to boil, then remove from heat. Stir in butter and vanilla; set aside. Sift flour, sugar, baking powder and salt together in medium bowl. Add milk, shortening and vanilla. Beat (med. speed) mixture for two minutes. Add egg; beat two more minutes. Pour into frozen pie shell, then stir chocolate sauce and pour over batter. Sprinkle with pecan pieces. Bake in preheated 350 oven for about an hour, or until pick or knife inserted in center comes out clean. Cool before cutting. Top with a dollop of whipped cream, if desired. Serves 8.

Vicksburg

Vicksburg has been called the "City of One Hundred Hills," but I think of this river city as "the cave town" because during the Civil War when Vicksburg was under seige, some local residents decided to seek higher, safer ground away from Yankee cannonballs. They moved their families into caves for the duration of the 47-day seige. One family welcomed a new baby who was born in a cave and named, appropriately, Seige Green.

The Vicksburg National Military Park is the nation's second largest, after Arlington. It's a poignant reminder of the war that pitted Americans against each other. The Visitor Center is where the tour begins, and it's where life-sized exhibitis and artifacts from the Siege of Vicksburg are on display. Civil War history is prominent in Vicksburg, some of which surrounds the Balfour House, built in 1835. The house was the site of a big Christmas Eve Ball that was interrupted by news that the Union army had penetrated the Confederate blockade, and thousands of troops were enroute to the city. The Confederate officers at the Balfour Ball bade their ladies farewell, and went off to fight.

While the war was in progress, Emma Balfour kept a diary of the Siege of Vicksburg, which proved to be an important historical document. She tells of watching mortars and parrot shells passing by her window, and how the Confederate soldiers were so exhausted trying to prevent General U.S. Grant from taking over the town. He finally did, on July 4, 1863, when Vicksburg surrendered. Union troops found a starving population and ragged, hungry, soldiers. The Confederates expected a celebration by the captors, though it was reported that the Federal troops provided much-needed food to the men who had gallantly defended Vicksburg.

When Grant and his troops marched in to take possession, they raised the Stars and Stripes over the Warren County Courthouse. According to legend, it was many years before Vicksburg celebrated the national holiday, Independence Day, on July 4th. Today, the Old Court House Museum, a National Historic Landmark, is a repository for old Mississippi history. It includes original Confederate flags, Jefferson Davis memorabilia, and other Civil War artifacts. It's also a tribute to the talents of the black craftsmen who helped construct it in 1858. Hear more about Vicksburg's history here; there's also a gift shop.

Here's a Mississippi story that I love. It cannot be substantiated, but it's made the rounds for a long time. Legend has it that in Bovina, a community near Vicksburg, on May 11, 1887, a most surprising and amazing object fell from the sky during a hail storm. The object of amazement was a 6"x8" gopher (turtle) that was solidly encased in ice. Supposedly, several people saw it before the ice melted. Earl's Art Gallery is also at Bovina. It's a workshop, gallery and museum that features the work of black Mississippi folk artist Earl Simmons. Similar folk art and exhibits may be seen at Margaret's Grocery, on Highway 61 just north of Vicksburg.

Riverboats docked on the Mississippi River.

Another interesting Vicksburg story involves the disappearance, in 1872, of the Iron Mountain, a 180 ft. paddlewheeler that left Vicksburg bound for New Orleans. Along with 55 passengers and a crew, the vessel was carrying a cargo of molasses and towing two barges loaded with cotton. Two hours after the Iron Mountain's departure, another steamer, the Iroquois Chief, almost collided with runaway cotton barges. Stories of the day said that the Iron Mountain simply vanished, leaving no survivors, no debris, and no clues.

Today, the relics of the past have made room for the Las Vegas-style casinos that are permanently docked on the Mississippi River. The glitz and glitter of the gambling "boats" light up the meandering old river --the same river that hosted the festive paddlewheelers in the earlier days of America.

Until not too long ago, there was a restaurant called the Old Southern Tea Room in an old hotel in Vicksburg. It was founded about 70 years ago by a real Southern belle named Mary McKay, a hostess of the first order. She initially shared her outstanding 'plantation delicacies' as a six-week tea room venture for tourists, though she later decided to remain open. She had little money, a wood-burning stove, and several generations of recipes, but she made a great success of her 'tea room' and a national name for herself. The restaurant was later owned by Mrs. Nancy Walker, who learned the art of great food and hospitality from Mrs. McKay.

Among the restaurant's most notable patrons was Duncan Hines, the cake mix connoisseur. It has been said that Hines once commented at a most impressive gathering that he would like to be at the Old Southern Tearoom in Vicksburg, Mississippi, enjoying the Stuffed Garden Eggplant and Corn Pudding.

I remember the white linen table cloths and the great food that was served, and I recall the disappointment I felt the first time I stopped there, enroute from Shreveport to Laurel, and it was closed. I salvaged a few recipes from this restaurant and a few others in Vicksburg; see below.

CHAMPAGNE PUNCH

3 quarts champagne
1 cup of rum
1 quart carbonated water
Frozen lemonade

Pour over two quart-blocks of frozen, unsweetened lemonade.

CHEESE BALLS

1-1/2 lbs. sharp Cheddar cheese, grated
1 small jar pimentoes, mashed
Mayonnaise (to soften)
About 1 cup ground peanuts

Mix above ingredients thoroughly; add red pepper and Worcestershire to taste and enough mayonnaise to make soft enough to roll into ball. Roll ball in ground peanuts.

OLD SOUTHERN "CAWN PUDDIN'"

1 can cream-style corn
1 tabsp. sugar
1 teasp. salt; pepper to taste
3 tabsp. butter, melted
5 eggs, well beaten
3 cups milk
1 tabsp. corn starch
1 tabsp. cold water

Combine first six ingredients. Dissolve corn starch in water and stir into corn mixture. Pour into a greased, shallow two quart baking dish. Bake at 350 degrees for about one hour, or until custard is firm. Serves 6.

ASPARAGUS CASSEROLE

1 can asparagus
4 hard-boiled eggs
1 can petit pois peas
1 can sliced mushrooms
1 can cream of mushroom soup
Squeeze of lemon juice
2 tabsp. melted butter
Toasted bread crumbs; paprika

Place asparagus crosswise in shallow, greased dish. Cover with sliced hard-boiled eggs, then a layer of peas. Drizzle melted butter over, then add a layer of mushrooms, a little lemon juice and mushroom soup. Top with toasted bread crumbs rolled in melted butter and paprika. Cook in moderate oven about 15 minutes. Serves 4 - 6.

POTATOES AU GRATIN

5 or 6 potatoes
Cream sauce
2 cups cream sauce
1/2 lb. grated sharp cheese

Cover whole peeled potatoes with boiling, salted water and cook about 35 minutes. Make cream sauce: 4 tablespoons butter, 4 tablespoons flour, 2 cups milk, salt and pepper to taste. Add half of cheese to sauce. Slice potatoes; place half in layer in casserole and cover with half of sauce. Add another layer of potatoes and sauce; cover top with remaining cheese. Bake at 375 degrees F. for 15 to 20 minutes. Serves 6.

DOWN IN DIXIE BOURBON PIE

21 marshmallows
1 cup evaporated milk
1/2 pint whipping cream
3 tabsp. bourbon
Crust (see below)
Whipped cream for topping

PIE: Melt marshmallows in undiluted milk, making sure not to boil. Chill. Whip cream and fold into marshmallow mixture. Add bourbon. Pour into cooled chocolate crumb crust and refrigerate 4 hours or until set. Top with whipped cream and chocolate crumbs.

CRUST: 1 box chocolate snaps, 1/2 cup melted butter (or margarine). Crush chocolate snaps; reserve some for topping. Mix the rest with melted butter. Pat into a 9-inch pie pan and bake until set. Cool and fill with pie mixture.

As the crow flies, if he flies slightly southwest, Vicksburg is not too far from Natchitoches (say Nak-a-tish), Louisiana, the neat and charming town on the Cane River. Therefore it's appropriate to use a favorite and famous Natchitoches delicacy in the Vicksburg recipes. We have it on good authority that the actors who came to Natchitoches to film *Steel Magnolias* had a fondness for these tasty morsels. This is an old recipe.

NATCHITOCHES MEAT PIES

For the Filling...

2 tabsp. shortening
2 tabsp. flour
1 cup onion, finely chopped
1 lb. lean ground pork, very lean
1 /2 lb. ground beef, very lean
1 bay leaf
1-1/2 teasp. black pepper
1-1/2 teasp. red pepper
1 cup celery, finely chopped
1/2 cup fresh parsley, chopped
1/2 cup bell pepper, chopped
2 cloves garlic, minced
1 to 2 tabsp. flour

For the Dough...

4 cups flour
3 teasp. baking powder
1 teasp. salt
1 tabsp. shortening
1 egg
1-1/3 cup milk

Heat the shortening in a black iron skillet. Add flour; brown. Add onion and cook until wilted, but do not brown. Stir in the pork, beef, and black and red pepper. Brown meat; simmer the mixture for 15 minutes. Skim off excess grease. Add remaining ingredients, except the flour. Simmer, low heat, for about 20 minutes. If too dry, add a little water. Sprinkle flour over mixture and stir until well blended, still at low heat. Cool the filling and refrigerate for several hours, even overnight.

In a large bowl mix together the dry ingredients. Cut shortening into the flour mixture; add the egg. Stir in enough milk to make a soft dough. Chill the dough for several hours, even overnight. Divide the dough into 2-inch balls. Place each ball of dough on a floured board and roll ball flat into a circle, about five inches in diameter. Place a heaping tablespoon of filling on 1/2 of the circle. Fold the dough over the filling, moisten the edges with water, then crimp together with a fork. In a deep fryer, fry the pies in deep fat (350 degrees) until light golden brown. Makes 35 pies. NOTE: Pies may be frozen after crimped, before frying.

ORANGE ROUGHY SUPREME

3 tabsp. green onions, chopped
2 teasp. fresh parsley, chopped
1 teasp. white wine Worcestershire
1/2 teasp. lemon zest
1/2 cup dry white wine
1 tabsp. fresh lemon juice
1 tabsp. almonds, chopped
2 teasp. constarch*
1/2 cup buttermilk
4 orange roughy fillets
Salt & pepper to taste
White wine (for boiling)
1 cup red grapes, seedless

Combine first six ingredients in a skillet; bring to a boil, reduce to about half a cup. Combine constarch with buttermilk; add to sauce and stir constantly until slightly thickened. Remove from fire. Preheat broiler, then salt and pepper fish fillets. Place fillets in baking dish and add white wine, about 2 teaspoons. Broil fish 3 to 5 minutes. Remove from broiler, pour sauce over fish, add grapes and sprinkle with almond pieces. Return to broiler and broil until sauce bubbles, about one minute. Serves 4. **May use one teaspoon arrowroot instead of cornstarch, according to preference.*

HAM AND CREOLE SAUCE FOR SUPPER

4 tabsp. butter
4 garlic cloves, minced
4 med. tomatoes, peeled and chopped
Red pepper and salt to taste
1-1/2 lb. ham steak
2 green onions, thinly sliced

Melt three tablespoons of butter over low heat; do not brown. Add garlic and stir; add chopped tomatoes and red pepper. Cook over low heat until tomatoes are somewhat soft and sauce is hot, about 10 to 12 minutes. In a large skillet, add and melt the remaining butter (1 tabsp.), and brown ham on both sides. Cook until heated through, just a few minutes. Arrange ham on platter, surrounded by tomato sauce, garnished on top with green onions. Serves 4.

STRAWBERRY ANGEL PARFAIT

1 pkg. strawberry gelatin
1 cup boiling water
1 pint vanilla ice cream
1 pkg. frozen strawberries
1 small angel food cake

Dissolve gelatine in juice from strawberries and 1 cup boiling water. Add vanilla ice cream. Stir until melted. Add strawberries and cake, which has been broken into small pieces. Chill until set. Slice in squares. Top with whipped cream.

KEY LIME PIE

4 eggs, separated
1 can condensed milk
1/3 cup lime juice (or lemon juice)
Pie shell

Beat the yolks of four eggs, and the white of one until thick. Add the condensed milk and beat again. Add the lime juice and stir until thick. Fold in the three remaining egg whites, which have been beaten dry. Pour into baked pie shell and cook in slow oven 15 minutes.

The Legend of the Singing River

It would be inappropriate to write about rivers in Mississippi and not mention the legend of the Singing River, a relatively short river in southeast Mississippi that runs into the Gulf of Mexico. It is officially named the Pascagoula River, and it is the swiftest river in this part of the state. The 81-mile long river varies from 50 to 300 yards wide and 10 to 30 feet deep, with many wide sandbars along the route. This river is the main stem of the hundreds of miles of channels, sloughs and oxbow lakes which comprise the wild and beautiful Pascagoula River Swamp and the Pascagoula Wildlife Management Area.

But it's the legend that captures the imagination. On a personal note, as a child, I spent many a night listening to the sounds when I went to the camphouse on the Pascagoula with my parents and our friends, and I could have sworn that I heard the eerie chant of the Pascagoula Indians. What I heard was an ominous sound --almost like a swarm of bees--but it was a sound of which I was not frightened. I remember it well to this day.

According to legend, a tragic event occurred at this river, an event which would today be considered mass suicide. The inhabitants of this region, the Pascagoula Indians, were gentle, innocent people who went about the business of feeding their families and carving out lives for themselves in the murky Pascagoula swampland. Their neighbors, the Biloxi tribe, called themselves the "first people" and they grew jealous of and antagonistic toward the Pascagoula. To make matters worse, a young princess of the Biloxi tribe fell in love with a young Pascagoula chieftain, even though she was betrothed to a Biloxi warrior. She fled to the Pascagoula tribe, and the Biloxi were further angered. Rather than fight and lose and face enslavement, the Pascagoula tribe joined hands and began a death chant as they walked into the deep waters. They sang until the last voice was hushed by the dark, engulfing waters. This story has been told and re-told, and to this date, there appears to be no scientific explanation for the sound that emanates from the Singing River. The sound is best heard during late summer and autumn.

The Tennessee-Tombigbee Waterway

We can't forget about America's newest river, the 234-mile long Tennessee-Tombigbee Waterway that connects middle America with the Gulf of Mexico. It was once the old Tombigbee River that ran through northcentral Mississippi. The Tenn-Tom, as it's called by those who know it well, was built and is maintained by the U.S. Army Corps of Engineers. This waterway, complete with an elaborate lock and dam system, represents the biggest project ever undertaken by the Army engineers. It also offers some of the best bass fishing in the country, according to various outdoor writers, as well as parks and campgrounds along its route through the clean and green northeast corner of Mississippi. Columbus is the biggest city on the Waterway.

Mississippi's other meandering rivers, to which settlers flocked, include the Pearl, the Wolf, Red Creek, the Tchoutacabouffa, the Bowie, the Chickasawhay, the Escatawpa, the Okatoma, the Bogue Chitto, the Homochitto, the Strong, the Yazoo, the Cold Water, the Big Black, the Leaf, the Chunky, the Sunflower, Bear Creek, the Tippah, the Tallahatchie, the Buttahatchee, the Noxubee, the Yalabusha, the Tangipahoa, which flows into Louisiana, and numerous tributaries, creeks, and bayous. Our rivers are the stuff of legends, for they all have stories of former glories.

The safe and scenic Tenn-Tom Waterway.

Mississippi cousins at the lake. "Don't we love our family reunions!"

Mississippi friends at a camphouse on the river.

Chapter 3
The Delta

Greenville

The Delta. Nothing else needs to be said. Those two words conjure up all sorts of images about this vast and interesting land. Writer David Cohn once said that the Mississippi Delta begins in the lobby of the Peabody Hotel in Memphis...and from there it runs a straight line almost to Vicksburg. Though Greenville is included in our River Towns section, it is very much a Delta town, too. Some say that Greenville is the heartbeat of the Delta, while smaller towns in the agriculturally-rich area serve as its soul.

There's no place like the Mississippi Delta. It is rich and poor, deadly quiet and juke joint noisy, sweaty hot in summer and windy cold in winter; it is laid back and intense, savvy and sleepy, and it is the ultimate contradiction. And even though the mighty Mississippi River is the lifeblood of this land, tiny back-waters meander through the Delta, some through the little towns that have a few old stores and not even a stoplight.

Delta hunter's haven.

Perhaps it's such contradictions that have inspired so many Delta writers of novels and song. Among the best known are Shelby Foote, William Alexander Percy, Ellen Douglas, Walker Percy, Bern Keating, Willie Morris, Beverly Lowry --and lesser known but equally as talented women writers include Louise Crump and Lucille Robinson Finlay. Crump's *Helen Templeton's Daughter* was widely acclaimed while Finlay --the first woman to be admitted to the Mississippi Bar Association wrote *The Coat I Wore*. See more about Delta writers at the Greenville Writer's Exhibit at the local library.

Familiar names that began in the Delta and are now well-known nationwide include the Steins of Greenville, the family who made SteinMart a favorite place to shop for most of America. Hodding Carter, Pulitzer Prize-winning journalist from Greenville, has a family with national political ties. Linton Weeks, editor of the great, late Southern Magazine, came from Clarksdale. The actress Carrie Nye, whose husband is talk-show host Dick Cavett, was once a Delta deb.

Others who call the Delta home include the talented actor Morgan Freeman, who still lives in the Delta when he's not on location for a film. As a matter of fact, Freeman owns a new restaurant in Clarksdale, Madidi's, and also a blues club called Ground Zero. Jim Henson, who created the Muppets, Kermit the Frog, Big Bird, and other animated characters who have delighted the children of America for decades, came from the Delta. A museum honoring his life and work is located on Deer Creek in Leland; it's The Birthplace of the Frog.

And then there's the music. Highway 61 is America's undisputed "Blues Highway." Numerous songs written by such blues legends as Son Thomas mention the Delta highway. Robert Johnson, Muddy Waters, John Lee Hooker, B.B. King, W.C. Handy, Charlie Patton, Howlin' Wolf, Mississippi John Hurt, and more have added to the Delta's music mystique. Singer Ike Turner, who was once the other half of Ike and Tina Turner, grew up in the Delta, as did Charley Pride, a favorite country music star who hails from the little town of Sledge. But it's Delta Blues that sets this region apart and has helped to garner the attention of the music world.

The Delta Blues Museum in **Clarksdale** has very good exhibits and serves as a repository for the Blues musicians so prominent in the region. The museum is housed in an old railway depot. It's a must-see for blues fans, and don't miss the life-size wax figure of Muddy Waters and his original cabin from the old Stovall Plantation.

Just outside of Clarksdale on Hwy. 49, find the Hopson Plantation and the completely unique Shack Up Inn. The inn consists of authentic sharecroppers' shacks from around the Delta, transplanted to the Hopson property and converted to overnight accommodations, complete with unexpected amenities. The exteriors are somewhat rickety and ramshackle by design, but the interiors are most comfortable. Unusual decorative items include a copper coil from a previous tenant's whiskey still, now recycled as a bathroom fixture.

Plans are in the works for an agricultural museum on Hopson Plantation --where the cotton picker was invented in 1944 -- and an arts center, which will feature the birth of the blues. Blues music has earned the interest of an international market, sure to be a boost to tourism in the Delta. Tourists appear to love the quirkiness of certain aspects of the Delta, including such unusual things as the commercial airliner sitting in the middle of a field. It actually sits on a lake, but from the highway, the lake can't be seen and the big commercial jet aircraft --probably a 747-- appears to be nesting in a cotton field. The aircraft now has a second life as the home of a Delta woman. Perhaps it could be called a non-mobile mobile home. Rumor has it that it's quite comfortable, complete with a Jacuzzi in the former cockpit.

Between Clarksdale to the north and Cleveland to the south, just off Highway 61, find the interesting little town of **Alligator**. The highway is in the process of being four-laned, so we hope that these interesting places will still be seen. If not, they may soon become extinct. Alligator sits beside Alligator Lake, a dark and mysterious bayou-type body of water, with cypress knees protruding from the murky depths. Alligator was once a thriving town that boasted about 20 stores, now it's virtually a vacant town surrounded by rich soil used for cotton farming and hunting. Alligator's claim to fame is that pioneer television producer Fred Coe (1914-1979) grew up here in a house now torn down. He produced such award-winning movies as *Marty, The Days of Wine and Roses, The Miracle Worker*, and more.

Cleveland has its share of blues, too, with a self-guided tour of important sites. Delta State University has interesting exhibits at the Fielding Wright Art Center, including a permanent collection that features the work of Salvador Dali. Cleveland has also been recognized as "One of the best small towns in America." Its downtown is about to get a new walking trail which was once a rail track, and that will only enhance the great shopping at about 40 downtown stores, known as the Cotton Row Shopping District.

Just north of Cleveland on Hwy. 61, the quaint little town of **Merigold** is a mecca for collectors of the wonderful pottery of Lee and Pup McCarty. What an interesting place! Walk through a bamboo tunnel to reach a garden filled with rare herbs, native plants and trees. A special treat is to have lunch there, which will be served on McCarty pottery.

A McCarty protege of many years has spun off and opened his own pottery in the nearby town of **Mound Bayou**. His work is superb, as you will see if you find and visit Peter's Pottery, along with the work of his talented brothers. The brothers sculpt crosses, animals, dinnerware and more using Mississippi clay and their own glaze, Bayou Blue. President George W. Bush has in his collection a Bayou Blue elephant. The quality of the work coming from McCarty Pottery and now Peter's Pottery, too, is legandary among Mississippi craftsmen.

Speaking of legends, parties in the Delta towns of **Greenville** and **Greenwood** have been known to reach legendary proportions. There's an old saying that Delta folks drink when the crops are bad, and when the crops are good. Any excuse to have a party is acceptable by Delta standards, from debutante balls to various festivals.

Delta hostesses have a good time when they entertain, and they say that it's quite possible to enjoy it as much as your guests do if you plan well and have good help. The secret, they say, is to select foods that can be prepared ahead of time. And never, never, try something new on guests. Their advice is to try a new dish on family, first.

The versatile staple, rice, is often served in the Delta, for rice fields are prominent sites on the landscape, sharing billing with Delta catfish farms. Many of the following recipes feature both these Delta delicacies, and the great pecans to be found around the region. Some recipes have a Louisiana flavor, since the two states are next door neighbors and share some of the same lifestyles and tastes.

ROASTED PECANS

1 quart pecan halves
1/2 stick butter or margarine
Salt, red pepper to taste

Place pecans in butter in heavy pan. Cook in 300 degree oven until pecans begin to brown. Stir lightly or shake occasionally to prevent burning. Remove from oven, pour out on wax paper, and add salt to taste. Red pepper may be used, as well. Cool and serve, or place in an airtight container to keep.

AVOCADO AND SHRIMP SPREAD

1 avocado, ripe and mashed
1 teasp. minced onion
1 teasp. lemon juice
Salt & pepper to taste
Party crackers, whole shrimp

Combine all ingredients until smooth. Spread on crackers and garnish with one whole shrimp in center. Quick and easy!

MUSHROOMS IN BURGUNDY WINE

1 cup burgundy wine
1 garlic clove, crushed
1 green onion, finely chopped
1/4 teasp. black pepper
1/3 cup butter, melted
1 container fresh mushrooms
1 teasp. minced parsley

Place first three ingredients in saucepan. Reduce liquid to 1/2 volume. Cool, then blend in pepper, minced parsley, and butter. Pan-broil mushrooms and cover with wine mixture. Serve hot in chafing dish.

RICE O'BRIEN

1 cup diced green pepper
1/4 cup butter or margarine
2 cups uncooked rice
4 cups chicken broth
2 teasp. salt
1 cup chopped pimento

Cook green pepper in butter until tender. Add rice, chicken broth, and salt. Heat to boiling; stir once. Cover, reduce heat, and simmer for 14 minutes, or until liquid is absorbed. Remove from heat and toss lightly with pimento. Serve hot; serves 8.

CATFISH ETOUFFEE

5 lbs. catfish, cut in large pieces
1/4 cup water
1 teasp. each salt and black pepper
1/4 teasp. red pepper
3 tabsp. salad oil
2 pods garlic, minced
1 bunch parsley, chopped
1 bell pepper, chopped
1 bay leaf
2 tabsp. flour
1/4 teasp. thyme
3 stalks celery, chopped
1 bunch green onions, chopped
1-1/2 cans tomato sauce
2 lemon slices

Rub fish pieces with a mixture of salt, black and red pepper. Place salad oil in bottom of black iron pot; arrange half the fish on the bottom. Mix chopped vegetables and sprinkle half over fish. Sprinkle one tablespoon flour over the vegetables and half of the tomato sauce; repeat layers. Add thyme, bay leaf, lemon slices and 1/4 cup water. Cook over low heat for about one hour. Shake pot often but do not stir; stirring breaks fish. Add more seasoning, according to preference. Serve over hot rice.

RIVER ROAD SEAFOOD CASSEROLE

1-1/2 lbs. shrimp, cooked, peeled
1 can crabmeat
3/4 cup celery, finely chopped
1/2 cup onion, chopped
1 cup mayonnaise
2 tabsp. Worcestershire
1/4 green pepper, finely chopped
Bread crumbs, about 1/2 cup

Mix all ingredients, then cover with buttered bread crumbs. Bake at 325 degrees for 25 minutes. Quick, easy, and good!

SMOTHERED QUAIL

6 quail, dressed
6 tabsp. butter
3 tabsp. flour
2 cups chicken broth
1/2 cup sherry (optional)
salt and pepper to taste
Cooked rice

Brown cleaned quail in butter in heavy skillet, then remove quail to baking dish. Add flour to butter in skillet and stir well. Slowly add chicken broth, sherry, salt and pepper. Blend well and pour over quail. Cover; bake at 350 degrees for about an hour, or until quail is tender. Serve over cooked rice, with gravy. Hot biscuits are a plus!

DELTA RICE AND BLACK BEAN SALAD

3 cups cooked rice
1 (16 oz.) can black beans, drained
1 med. red bell pepper, chopped
1 med. green bell pepper, chopped
4 green onions, chopped
1/4 cup fresh cilantro
1/3 cup peanut oil
1/4 cup lime juice
large lettuce leaves
2 avocados, peeled and sliced

In a large bowl, combine the first six ingredients. In a small bowl, whisk together oil and lime juice. Pour over rice mixture; mix lightly but well. Add salt, black and red pepper to taste. Cover and refrigerate. Serve in mounds on large lettuce leaves; garnish with avocado slices. Serves 6.

GREEN BEANS SUPREME

2 cans whole green beans
1 can bean sprouts
1 can water chestnuts, sliced
1 cup chopped celery
1 cup chopped bell pepper
1 large onion, sliced thin

Mix these ingredients with 3 tablespoons salad oil. In separate bowl mix 1 cup vinegar, 1/2 cup water, 3/4 cup sugar, and 3 teaspoons salt. Mix well and pour over salad, then refrigerate. Serve as a salad or cold vegetable; serves 6.

CREAMED CAULIFLOWER

2 lbs. cauliflower
2 slices bread
2 cups milk
1/2 stick butter or margarine, melted
1/2 lb. cheddar cheese, sliced thin
1/2 cup chopped onions
1/2 cup chopped celery
Salt and pepper to taste
Red pepper to taste

Remove crust from bread and discard. Soak remaining bread in milk for about ten minutes. Add melted butter, onions and celery. Season to taste, then cook over medium heat until a thick cream gravy is formed. In uncovered pot, cook cauliflower in enough boiling water to cover it, for about 20 minutes. Drain well, cut up cauliflower, and cover with cream gravy. Place thin slices of cheese on top; bake at 350 degrees until cheese melts. Serves 8.

PECAN PIE

1/2 cup butter or margarine
3/4 cup light brown sugar
2 tabsp. flour
3 eggs, slightly beaten
1 cup light Karo syrup
Dash of salt
1 teasp. vanilla
1 cup pecans
1 pie shell, unbaked (9 inch)

Cream together the butter, brown sugar, and flour. Add eggs, beat mixture until smooth. Mix in the syrup, salt and vanilla. Spread the pecans in the bottom of the unbaked pie shell and pour the mixture over them. Bake the pie at 350 degrees for 45 minutes. Cool for about an hour. Serves 6 to 8.

AUNT DELIA'S DELIGHTFUL DESSERT

3/4 stick butter or margarine
1 cup coconut (Angel Flake)
1 cup chocolate morsels (old kind)
1 cup chopped pecans
1 cup Graham cracker crumbs
1 can condensed milk

Mix together first five ingredients, then pat into greased, 9x13 baking dish. Pour condensed milk over all. Bake at 350 degrees for about 30 minutes, or until firm. Cut into small squares; top with whipped cream. So easy, and good!

Greenwood

Greenwood is not without its Delta ambiance, though it is located at the eastern gateway to the Delta. Greenwood is the self-proclaimed cotton capital of the world, which may be why it's home to the Cottonlandia Museum, where cotton agriculture is prominently displayed. Sharing billing with cotton is a mastadon skeleton, the work of contemporary Mississippi artists, and an exhibit called "Delta Swamp." The Malmaison Room shows the opulent lifestyles of Delta planters.

Greenwood is also home to the Florewood River Plantation, a full-scale replica of an 1850s cotton plantation, complete with fields in cultivation, pastureland, barns, blacksmith shop, and "the Big House." Florewood is a Mississippi State Park that is also a living history museum. A gift shop is on the premises.

The city of Greenwood is named for the part Choctaw, part Frenchman named Greenwood LeFleur, later changed to Leflore, who became chief of the Choctaw tribe at the age of 25. Leflore, born in 1800, was in later life elected to the state legislature and he also became a prosperous Delta planter. His massive plantation, Malmaison, burned in 1942. The late Greenwood Leflore remains one of Mississippi's most colorful historical figures.

Between Greenwood and Greenville, the small town of **Indianola** is the hometown of bluesman B.B. King and noted chef and author Craig Claiborne. Claiborne's mother ran a boarding house from their Southern Colonial-style home at 208 West Percy Street. Mrs. Claiborne was a legendary cook and hostess in the Delta. Her son Craig became the popular food editor and columnist for *The New York Times.* He was the author of eight best-selling cookbooks and an autobiography entitled, *A Feast Made for Laughter.*

Claiborne once said that though his mother considered catfish "common," he personally believed it to be..."The finest freshwater fish in America, on the way to becoming haute cuisine." The celebrated chef developed several recipes using the Delta-grown catfish. Today, Delta catfish farms supply about 75 percent of the nation's catfish consumption.

Following are two recipes with a distinctly Southern flavor that were found among Craig Claiborne's recipe books. They may not be the down-home cookin' that is standard fare throughout the Magnolia State, but sure to be delicious.

RED BEANS & RICE

2 cups dried red or kidney beans
1-1/2 cup thinly sliced Polish sausage
1-1/2 cup thinly sliced leeks
1-1/2 cups chopped fennel bulb, if available
1/2 teasp. dried thyme
Salt to taste
1 small dried hot red pepper, crushed
1 tabsp. vinegar
1 cup rice
2-1/4 cups chicken broth
1/2 cup finely chopped parsley
1/2 teasp. lemon juice
1/2 teasp. salt
1 cup diced, cooked chicken
Chopped green pepper, optional

1. Soak the beans overnight in cold water to cover.
2. Drain the beans and add enough cold water to cover to a depth of one inch above the tops of the beans. Add the sausage, leeks, fennel, thyme, salt, pepper, and vinegar. Cover and cook until beans are done and most of the liquid has been absorbed. Add more liquid as necessary or uncover to reduce the amount of liquid.
3. Meanwhile, combine the rice with the broth, parsley, lemon juice, salt, and chicken. Cover and bring to the boil. Cook until all the liquid is absorbed, 12 to 14 minutes.
4. Combine the rice and beans and serve hot garnished with chopped green peppers (or chopped green onion tops). Yield: 6 to 8 servings.

CORNMEAL FRITTERS WITH LEFTOVERS

1 cup yellow cornmeal
1/4 cup flour
1/2 teasp. baking powder
1/2 teasp. salt
1/2 teasp. freshly ground black pepper
1/8 teasp. cayenne
1-1/4 cup boiling chicken broth
3/4 cup finely diced leftover meat and/or chopped green onions
Oil

1. In a mixing bowl, combine the cornmeal, flour, baking powder, salt, pepper, and cayenne. Add the boiling broth gradually, stirring constantly. Stir in the meat and/or vegetables.
2. Heat just enough oil on a griddle or in a black iron skillet to prevent the fritters from sticking. Drop the batter by spoonfuls onto the griddle and cook, turning as the fritters are browned on one side, like pancakes. Cook until browned on the second side and serve, if desired, with hot pepper jelly. Yield: 12 to 20 fritters, depending on size.

Craig Claiborne said in a previous interview that the meal he remembered and loved most from his childhood was his mother's chicken spaghetti. The recipe and notes he used in a book covered three pages, so the recipe here is not his, but it is an excellent recipe nevertheless. None of the following recipes can be attributed to Claiborne; just the two above.

CHICKEN SPAGHETTI

1 large, fat hen
2 large onions, chopped
3 cloves garlic, minced
4 stalks celery, chopped
1 bell pepper, chopped
1 bunch green onions, chopped
1/2 bunch parsley, chopped
2 tabsp. bacon drippings
1 can tomato sauce
1 can tomato soup
1/2 small can tomato paste
Salt and pepper to taste
1 bay leaf
Dash of Louisiana Hot Sauce
2 tabsp. Worcestershire sauce
2 cups chicken broth

Boil hen in water seasoned with salt and pepper to taste. Save broth; should be at least two cups. Remove chicken meat from bones and cut into large pieces; set aside. In large, heavy pot, sauté next five ingredients in hot bacon drippings, adding parsley as this cooks. Add next seven ingredients. Thin mixture with broth and add chicken. Cover and simmer for about one hour, until sauce has thickened. Serve over thin spaghetti. Serves 6.

CATFISH COURTBOUILLON

(Cajuns say "Coo-be-yonh")

This calls for a roux, and there's a secret to roux-making. Put the cup of oil in a heavy iron pot and heat on medium. When oil is hot, gradually add one cup flour, stirring constantly. When oil and flour are combined, lower heat and continue to stir constantly until golden brown, about the color of coffee with cream. The addition of onions, celery, or bell peppers will keep roux from burning. Remove from heat and pour into another container immediately so that roux won't become too dark.

4 lbs. catfish fillets
1 cup cooking oil
1 cup flour
1 cup chopped onions
1/2 cup chopped celery
1/2 cup chopped bell pepper
4 cloves minced garlic
1 can whole tomatoes (16 oz.)
1 can tomato paste (12 oz.)
2 quarts cold water
Salt and black pepper to taste
Red pepper to taste

Cut fish into three-inch pieces. Season with salt and peppers; set aside. Make roux, adding onions, celery, bell pepper. Cook over medium heat until vegetables are wilted, continuing to stir constantly. Add tomato paste, tomatoes, and 2 cups cold water. Continue to cook over medium heat, uncovered, until tomatoes and oil separate, about 40 minutes, then add minced garlic.

Add two quarts of water, bring to a boil, boil gently for about 30 minutes, then add fish. Cook for another 30 minutes over medium heat. Serve over hot cooked rice. Serves 8.

BAKED CHICKEN TARRAGON

8 chicken breast halves, skinned, boned
Salt and pepper to taste
3 tabsp. lemon juice
1/2 cup mayonnaise
1 cup celery, finely chopped
1 teasp. dried tarragon
1 lb. fresh spinach
3 med. tomatoes, cut, wedged

Sprinkle chicken with salt and pepper. Arrange in 13 x 9 pan; sprinkle with lemon juice. Bake at 375 degrees for 30 minutes, or until done, then set aside to cool.

Combine mayonnaise, celery and tarragon; set aside. Remove stems from spinach; wash leaves thoroughly, then drain, patting dry. Arrange spinach on serving plates, then place chicken and tomato wedges on top of spinach leaves. Spoon mayonnaise mixture over chicken. Garnish with celery leaves, if you wish. Serves 8. For a luncheon salad, coarsely chop cooked chicken and combine it with mayonnaise mixture.

BAKED WILD RICE

2 cups uncooked wild rice
1 can tomatoes
1 teasp. butter
1/2 lb. sharp cheese, grated
12 stuffed olives
2 large cans whole mushrooms
Salt and pepper to taste

Use butter to grease 9x12 inch baking dish. Add all other ingredients; mix well. Cook at 350 degrees for 1-1/2 hours. Sprinkle extra cheese on top when done. Serves 12.

ASPARAGUS AMANDINE

2 cans asparagus spears, drained (save liquid)
1 can cream of mushroom soup
1/2 cup liquid from asparagus
1/2 teasp. salt
1/4 teasp. pepper
1 cup bread crumbs
4 tabsp. butter, melted
1 cup Cheddar cheese, grated
1/2 cup blanched almonds

Place asparagus in oblong casserole. Cover with mushroom soup mixed with liquid, salt and pepper. Sprinkle with grated cheese. Add bread crumbs to melted butter and sprinkle over grated cheese. Dot with almonds. Bake at 350 degrees for 45 minutes. Serves about 8.

ENCORE CABBAGE

2 med. cabbages, cored and quartered
1/2 cup butter
2 med. onions, chopped
1 bell pepper, chopped
3 cloves garlic, minced
1/2 lb. Velveeta cheese
Salt and pepper to taste
1 cup bread crumbs
1/2 pint Half & Half cream
2 tabsp. grated Cheddar cheese

Boil the cabbage in small amount of water until tender. Drain, cool, and chop finely. Melt butter over medium heat, then add onion and sauté until wilted. Add bell pepper, garlic, and cabbage and continue to cook until the bell pepper is tender. Stir in Velveeta, salt, pepper (a sprinkle of red pepper adds interest) and one half of the bread crumbs; continue stirring until cheese melts. Place this mixture in a 2-qt. buttered casserole; add the cream. Combine other half of bread crumbs with the Cheddar cheese; cover casserole with this mixture. Bake at 350 degrees for about 15 minutes, or until bubbly. Serves 8 to 10.

CHEESY SQUASH

1 lb. yellow squash
2 eggs, beaten
1/4 cup onion, finely chopped
1/2 teasp. sage
1 cup grated Cheddar cheese
1/2 teasp. salt, pepper to taste
Paprika

Steam squash until tender; drain. Blend together the squash, eggs, onion, sage, one half of the cheese, and salt and pepper. Pour the mixture into a greased casserole. Sprinkle with paprika and remaining half of cheese. Bake at 350 degrees for about 25 minutes. Serves 4.

COTTON PICKIN' GREAT CAKE

1 box butter cake mix, any brand
4 eggs
1/2 cup cooking oil
1 cup pecans, finely chopped
1 can Mandarin orange slices (save juice)

CAKE: Combine first four ingredients; mix. Add the Mandarin orange slices and juice; stir by hand. Pour the batter into three, well-greased 9-inch cake pans and bake at 350 degrees for 35 minutes. Cool layers, then ice with Cotton Pickin' Frosting, below.

FROSTING: In a large bowl, use fork to mix 1 can (20 oz.) crushed pineapple, with juice; 1 (6 oz.) package instant vanilla pudding mix; 1 (9 oz.) carton Kool Whip. Spread the frosting between layers and on the top and sides of the cake; refrigerate.

TIPSY PUDDIN'

1 pkg. unflavored gelatin
1/4 cup cold water
2 cups milk, hot but not boiled
2 egg yolks, slightly beaten
1/2 cup sugar
1/2 cup sherry
2 egg whites, beaten 'til stiff
1 cup whipping cream, whipped
2 dozen ladyfingers, split

In bowl, soften gelatin in water. Stir in milk, egg yolks, sugar, and sherry. Chill mixture until it begins to congeal, then fold in the beaten egg whites and whipped cream. Line a 2-quart bowl with ladyfingers. Add alternate layers of the gelatin mixture and ladyfingers. Chill for a minimum of 8 hours. Serves about 8.

MISSISSIPPI MUD CAKE

1 cup Wesson oil
1/2 cup cocoa
4 eggs
1-3/4 cup sugar
1-1/2 cup flour, self-rising
2 teasp. vanilla
2 cups chopped pecans

CAKE: Mix all ingredients; pour in 9x13 inch pan and bake at 300 degrees for 30 to 45 minutes. Cover with small marshmallows when removed from oven. Mix icing and pour over cake while still warm.

ICING: Mix these ingredients and pour over cake: 1-1/2 sticks margarine, 1 tablespoon vanilla, 1 box powdered sugar, 1/3 cup cocoa, 1/2 cup Pet milk, 1/2 cup chopped nuts.

Elsewhere in the Delta, old towns and interesting sites are just down the road a mile or two. Expect to see big catfish farms, for this is indeed catfish country. You'll find good things in and around **Belzoni**, among them The Catfish Capitol, a museum dedicated to the tasty fish. Learn about catfish farming, as they say, "from pond to plate," and see the work of Mississippi artists who exhibit ceramics, metals, and more.

Belzoni is also the home of "Mama's Dream World," the Ethel Wright Mohamed Stitchery Museum. Mrs. Mohamed charted the growth of her family -- and the Delta-- in intricate stitchery. When the artist Mohamed died in 1992 at the age of 85, she had created about 200 needlework pictures. Outdoor lovers will find their way to Wister Gardens, a 14-acre wonderland developed by Frances Chiles Henry and Wister Henry, beginning around 1937. Flowering fruit trees, crape myrtles, thousands of rose bushes and azaleas, and a six-sided gazebo.

Yazoo City is also a gateway town to the Delta, though it's a place with an identity all its own. You may be familiar with it, thanks to Yazooan Willie Morris, who wrote about the town in his books, *Good Old Boy* and *My Dog Skip*. Morris's books and films made Yazoo City appear to be the best possible place to have grown up, even with --or perhaps because of-- such inspiring tales as *The Witch of Yazoo* who, according to legend, threatened in 1884 to "...burn the whole town down on the morning of May 25, 1904." Those were the last words she said before she sank into quicksand and died. Townspeople removed her body the next day and buried her in the center of the town cemetery, with heavy chains placed around her grave.

This is a fact: On May 25, 1904, the town of Yazoo was relegated to ashes, with "Flames leaping three blocks at a time" when the predicted fire raced through the town. After the fire, a few townspeople went to the Glenwood Cemetery and found that the witch's chains had been broken as if by supernatural strength. And it is a fact that the town was re-built within a year, which says so much about the spirit of the people of Yazoo. No wonder the town nurtured the imagination of the late, great, Mississippi writer Willie Morris. Other well-known native Yazooans are the late comedian Jerry Clower, motivational speaker Zig

Florewood River Plantation State Park is a living recreation of Delta plantation life in the 1850s. Tour the 'big house' and hear about the daily activities, from teaching to weaving, to canning and cooking. Also on site is a blacksmith shop, a plantation store, a school, and other buildings in which demonstrations are on-going at certain times of the year. As you enter the park, don't miss the Cotton Museum and gift shop. The plantation/park is two miles west of Greenwood, just off Highway 82.

Ziglar, politicians Haley Barbour and Mike Espy, among others.

Yazoo City is also the home of The Oakes African-American Cultural Center. The grand old Victorian was the home of the Oakes family for 125 years. From its austere beginnings as a one-room structure when the Oakes came from South Carolina and bought it in 1866, it is now a big, fully restored house that is listed on the National Register of Historic Places. Today it is a museum that houses a wealth of information about African-American history and culture.

Kudzu taking an artistic form in the Delta.

Delta Blues Museum, Clarksdale.

Chapter 4
North Mississippi and The Hill Country

North Mississippi is a clean and green region of rolling hills and lush forests. Here you'll find such idyllic towns as **Oxford**, home of the state's esteemed Ole Miss; **Starkville**, where Mississippi State University rules the roost, and **Columbus**, where Mississippi University for Women --the W-- has educated the state's genteel young women --now smart men, too-- since 1884.

The towns of **Southaven, Hernando** and **Olive Branch** are practically bedroom communities for nearby Memphis, Tennessee, but Mississippi is pleased to call them our own. Olive Branch's Old Towne Business District has a large selection of antique and specialty shops, while Hernando's downtown area tells about the cross-through of explorer Hernando DeSoto at the Historic Museum and the Courthouse.

Batesville boasts a quaint, interesting downtown, where Victorian houses and old store fronts could be taken from a movie lot. Shoppers flock to the factory outlet stores at Batesville, about 31 in all, to spend the day finding bargains. Outdoor lovers, the big Sardis Lake welcomes you. Batesville is the hometown of Governor Ronnie Musgrove.

The venerable **Holly Spring**s, in the extreme northwest corner of the state, is one of the Mississippi treasures we hold near and dear. It's a lovely town with many old mansions lining the streets, and a Civil War history sccond to none. The town was occupied by Union troops, with General and Mrs. U.S. Grant taking up residence at the Walter Place, one of the town's prominent antebellum homes best known today for its octagonal battlement towers. It has been said that the town was spared from burning because some of the townspeople had been cordial to the wife of the Yankee general.

Holly Springs must have been inspiring to writers and artists, for many hail from here. Among the best known are the Episcopal priest and prolific novelist Joseph Holt Ingraham. He began writing romantic novels, and later wrote a trilogy of religious novels, including the widely-read *The Prince of the House of David,* a fictional account of the life of Christ. Ingraham was born in Maine, but a Mississippian by choice and by marriage. His last book was published just before the Civil War; it was written to promote a better understanding of the South. He died in 1860 after having written about 100 books.

The young artist Kate Freeman Clark left Holly Springs at age 16 -- escorted by her mother-- to study painting in New York City with famed artist William Merritt Chase. Upon their return to Holly Springs, Clark began painting fast and furiously. She had painted about 1,000 paintings prior to 1914. At her death in 1957, her paintings were still unsold and virtually unseen, by choice. Today, the Kate Freeman Clark Art Gallery is open by appointment.

The legendary Phillips Restaurant and Grocery Store, across from the train station, is known for outstanding, old-fashioned hamburgers and fried peach turnovers. Checker boards have bottlecaps for checker pieces, and they still sell one cent candy. Don't miss the Marshall County Historical Museum and its fine collection of Civil War memorabilia. It will remind you of ferreting out treasures in your grandmother's attic.

Holly Springs has an Elvis connection, too, one that's an unusual tribute to the king of rock and roll. It's called Graceland Too, and it began as a part of the Elvis collection of the self-proclaimed "World's ultimate number one Elvis fans," the father and son team of Paul McLeod and Elvis Aaron Presley McLeod. Yes, the son is named for Elvis. The extensive memorabilia includes original records, photographs, movie posters, and thousands of newspaper clippings about the original Elvis.

Elvis has a connection to the next town, too. Rumor has it that he was scheduled to appear in Corinth in 1954, but had to cancel the performance due to slow ticket sales! It must have been just afterward that he jolted conservative north Louisiana with his music and methods of expressing himself, namely his gyrations. He was an unprecedented hit at the Louisiana Hayride near Shreveport, which soon started packing in the Elvis fans.

Corinth

Corinth, across the state in the upper northeast corner, is another town filled with history and Old South traditions. Lovely homes are abundant, and Corinth boasts a downtown business center that includes the state's oldest drugstore, Borroum's, which is still in operation today and still in the same family. The pharmacist who runs the drug store, Camille Borroum Mitchell, is the great granddaughter of Dr. A. J. Borroum, the former Confederate Army surgeon who built the business in 1869. A fine collection of Native American and Civil War artifacts are on display at Borroum's, and there's also a soda fountain where you can still get a fountain Coca-Cola and catch up on the latest happenings in Corinth.

The Northeast Mississippi Museum does a good job of telling the Corinth story, beginning with Corinth's pivotal role in the Civil War. As a railroad town where several lines intersected, Corinth was strategically important to both armies of the war. More than 6,000 soldiers are interred at the National Cemetery, which was once a battlefield. The Corinth Civil War Interpretive Center has a video and maps for a walking tour of this lovely old town.

Some of the state's best known writers and musicians hail from North Mississippi, among them William Faulkner, Pulitzer Prize-winning author from Oxford. Elvis Presley, the world's undisputed king of rock and roll, is a native of Tupelo; Tennessee Williams, Pulitzer Prize-winning playwright for *A Streetcar Named Desire* and *Cat on a Hot Tin Roof,* was born in Columbus. Currently, the world's best-selling author claims this region, too, and he is John Grisham.

Oxford

Both William Faulkner and John Grisham had ties to the University of Mississippi in Oxford, the state's own Ole Miss. It's a place to behold on its own, even without the connection to several best-selling authors. Ole Miss boasts the Barnard Observatory, the Lyceum, the Center for the Study of Southern Culture, the Blues Archives --said to house the world's largest collection of Delta blues music-- and the University Museums. The latter also manages Rowan Oak, Faulkner's home on Old Taylor Road.

If you're a fan of the South, you're probably familiar with the Southern studies going on at Barnard Observatory, where the Center for the Study of Southern Culture is housed. Since 1977, this innovative group has put a positive spin on anything Southern. The university helps to call attention to its literary prowess with the annual Faulkner and Yoknapatawpha Conference held each summer. Different themes apply, from Faulkner and gender to Faulkner and culture. Fans and scholars come from everywhere to attend this stellar event, and also the Oxford Conference for the Book.

Downtown Oxford is an attraction, as well. The Oxford Square came into being in 1835, when three men built a log cabin and opened a general store atop a hill. They decided to call the town "Oxford," after the city in England that holds a great university. Eleven years later, Mississippi's Oxford had its own esteemed university.

Colonel Reb

Today the Square is the center of activity for the town of Oxford, with most everything else in close proximity. Big, shady trees keep the Square pleasant even on a hot summer day. The state's oldest department store, Neilsens, is located on the square, and it continues to offer quality merchandise. Square Books is one of the South's best bookstores. If you're interested in Southern writers, this is the place to find them. There's a great balcony from which to read or view the town.

And under the big, shady trees of the Grove on the Ole Miss campus is the place to be during the fall, when SEC football games are played on campus. Though some of the tailgate parties are elaborate productions that would make Hollywood take note, others are more laid-back and casual. Some of the following recipes will be found served-up on sterling --or maybe styrofoam-- depending upon the preference of the tailgaters and the temperature. Football games start while it's still hot and humid, so plan your tailgate parties accordingly.

MUSHROOM CANAPES

2 tabsp. butter or margarine
1 sm. pkg. fresh mushrooms, chopped
1 (8 oz.) pkg. cream cheese, cubed, soft
1 tabsp. dry white wine
1 teasp. lemon juice
1/4 teasp. garlic powder
1/8 teasp. hot sauce
16 white bread slices

At Home: Melt butter in skillet; add mushrooms, saute about 10 minutes. Process cream cheese and next four ingredients in a blender or food processor until smooth. Stir in mushrooms, and chill at least two hours. **At The Grove:** cut bread slices with a 2-inch cutter, then spread mushroom mixture on bread. Garnish with a sprig of parsley, if desired. Makes about 32 appetizers.

D's CHEESE STRAWS

1 lb. sharp cheddar cheese, grated
1-1/2 cups all-purpose flour
1/4 cup butter, softened
1 teasp. salt
1/4 teasp. red pepper

Process all ingredients in a food processor for about 30 seconds, until mixture forms a ball. Use a cookie press fitted with a star-shaped disc to shape mixture into straws; place on ungreased cookie sheets and bake at 375 degrees until lightly browned. Cool on wire racks. Makes about 8 dozen straws.

SPINACH DIP

1 (10-oz.) box frozen, chopped spinach
1 pkg. Knorr's vegetable soup mix
1 cup sour cream
1 cup mayonnaise
1 can water chestnuts, chopped
4 green onions, chopped

Cook spinach; drain, squeeze thoroughly. Mix all ingredients and chill for several hours, preferably day before. Serve with crackers or Melba toast.

MARINATED VEGETABLES

1 small container fresh mushrooms
1 can (14 oz.) artichoke hearts, drained
1 can (6 oz.) pitted ripe olives, drained
1/2 cup vegetable oil
1/4 cup olive oil
1/2 cup lemon juice
1/3 cup finely chopped onion
1 teasp. salt
1/4 teasp. pepper
3 bay leaves
1 tabsp. chopped fresh parsley

Clean mushrooms with damp cloth; trim. Combine mushrooms with artichokes and olives, then set aside. Combine vegetable oil and remaining ingredients in a jar. Close tightly and shake vigorously. Pour marinade over vegetables. Cover and refrigerate at least 12 hours. Drain vegetables and discard bay leaves. Serves 8.

ROASTED CHICKEN SALAD

2 cups chopped, cooked chicken
1/2 cup seedless grapes, halved
1/2 cup chopped pecans, toasted
1/4 cup mayonnaise
2 tabsp. sour cream
1 tabsp. fresh lime juice
Lettuce leaves
Pita bread rounds

Combine first three ingredients in a medium bowl. Combine mayonnaise, sour cream, and lime juice; stir into chicken mixture. Serve on lettuce leaves, or stuff in pita bread rounds which have been lined with lettuce. Serves about 4; easily doubled.

HAM AND POTATO SALAD

1 lb. small red potatoes, cut into 1/2 inch wedges
1 (16 oz.) pkg. froxen mixed vegetables
1/3 cup mayonnaise
1/3 cup sour cream
1/2 cup chopped green onions
1 teasp. pepper
1/2 teasp. salt
3 cups (1 lb.) cooked, chopped ham

Cook potatoes, covered, in boiling water about 10 minutes or until tender. Drain and set aside. Cook frozen mixed vegetables according to package directions; drain and set aside. Combine mayonnaise and next four ingredients in large bowl. Gently stir in potatoes, vegetables, and ham. Cover and refrigerate overnight. Serves 6 to 8.

HONEY PECAN CHICKEN

4 sticks butter or margarine
2 cups honey
1/2 cup fresh lemon juice
1 cup chopped pecans
8 to 10 boneless chicken breasts
Pecan halves

Cook chicken breasts (no skin) in oven, at 350 degrees for one hour. In saucepan, combine first four ingredients. Simmer for about 35 to 40 minutes until sauce is thick. To serve, place chicken on platter; top with honey pecan sauce; garnish with lightly toasted pecan halves. Serves 8.

GROVE RICE PILAU

- 1/2 stick butter or margarine
- 1 cup raw rice
- 2 cups chicken broth
- 1/2 teasp. salt, pepper to taste
- 1/2 cup stuffed olives
- 1/2 cup chopped green pepper
- 1/2 cup sliced mushrooms, fresh

Melt butter, add rice and stir. Saute 5 - 8 minutes, stirring constantly. Rice needs to be a light brown color. Stir in chicken broth, salt and pepper. Add next three ingredients. Bake at 350 degrees for 1/2 hour covered, then stir and bake 1/2 hour uncovered. Serves about 6; doubles nicely.

Elsewhere in North Mississippi, expect to find a plethora of casinos around **Tunica, Lula,** and **Robinsonville**, near Memphis. You'll think you've arrived in Las Vegas, with all the glitz and glitter of shore-docked "gambling boats." They come laden with their own restaurants, hotels, and all the amenities. Big-name entertainers appear often; you may want to call for specific details and entertainment agenda. Not too far off the beaten path is Moon Lake, made famous in writings by William Faulkner and Tennessee Williams as the Moon Lake Casino. Look for it near the town of **Dundee.**

New Albany is actually the birthplace of novelist William Faulkner, though his formative years were spent in Oxford. Situated on the Tallahatchie River, this town offers the Union County Heritage Museum and nature walks along the river. Remember the old Bobbie Gentry song about Billy Joe McAllister throwing something off the Tallahatachie Bridge?

Tupelo

And then there's Tupelo, the birthplace of Elvis Presley, the loose-hipped singer known the world over as the king of rock 'n roll. Tupelo is a family-oriented town of excellent schools and churches, and about the friendliest people in the state. Tupelo appears to be innocent of history, for there are few mid-1800s monuments to serve as reminders of war and wasted lives, though Tupelo did see Civil War action on its turf. Most of the town's notoriety centers around Elvis.

Pre-Elvis, there was the colorful "Private" John Allen, who began his career in the U.S. House of Representatives in 1884. His moniker, "Private" Allen, came about when Allen quipped that everyone who had served in 'the (Civil) War' had been nothing less than a brigadier general, but that he was proud that he'd been a private. It was Allen who asked Congress to establish a fish hatchery in Tupelo, which is still in service today.

Tupelo's Own Elvis Presley

Being at the Elvis Presley birthplace, park, and museum leads to a better understanding of this man who changed the way the world heard music. The "shotgun" house, about the size of a railroad caboose, was built by Elvis's father Vernon and Vernon's father for about $180, which Vernon borrowed. Built the year Elvis was born, Vernon and Gladys moved in to await the birth of their baby, though two were born on Januray 8, 1935. Elvis Aaron had a still-born twin named Jesse Garon.

Times were hard during those Depression years, and when Elvis was three years old the Presley's were evicted from the house they'd built because they couldn't re-pay the loan. The family continued to live in Tupelo until Elvis was 13 years old, when they moved to Memphis and he began to take his music quite seriously. The doe-eyed teenager with a guitar, long hair and colorful clothing stood out in the crowd of crew cuts, t-shirts, and jeans. When he sang, his unusual way of dress was forgotten, for here was a young man who sang a combination of blues and spirituals, with an unusual rhythm, unforgettable lyrics, and an unorthodox way of moving his body to keep time with the beat of the music. It was the kind of music that demanded --and got-- movement.

Still today, his birthplace in Tupelo attracts thousands of visitors per year and the home he bought in Memphis, Graceland, attracts thousands per day. Fans often wait in line to buy tickets to Graceland, then take a tram across the street to partake of a guided tour of Graceland and its grounds. The tours are very specific, from memorized recitations by tour guides, to absolutely no variance in what to see in what order.

But the Tupelo birthplace is the one that offers an opportunity for quieter reflection, according to serious Elvis fans. More than 20,000 fans per years experience the Elvis aura at the little shotgun house that his father built. When Elvis was 21 and had already earned fame and money, he came back to Tupelo to perform at the big Mississippi-Alabama Fair. The rising rock 'n roll star donated his share of the proceeds to start a park in his hometown. With the help of the city of Tupelo and fans, the Elvis Presley Park was born. The house was renovated and opened in 1971.

Though Elvis became a superstar, those who knew him best say that deep-down, he remained an humble, well-mannered, country boy who loved his mother and honored his father, always. And he apparently touched the hearts of millions along the way.

Elvis's favorite food was said to be a fried peanut butter and banana sandwich, but we have it on good authority that he liked plain old-fashioned Southern cookin', too, from biscuits and red-eye gravy to barbecue and collard greens. He had a fondness for barbecue and simple, unadorned meat loaf, which are two of the 'Elvis inspired' recipes below. Other recipes represent the taste of Tupelo.

BARBECUED PORK

Pork butt roast, about 2-1/2 lbs.
1 teasp. corn oil
1 (4 oz.) can tomato sauce
1/4 cup cider vinegar
Big dash Worcestershire sauce
1/4 cup brown sugar
Salt and pepper to taste
1/2 cup celery seeds
Chili powder to taste
Red pepper to taste

Pierce meat with knife several times. Place in dutch oven, and brown on all sides in corn oil. In a separate bowl, combine other ingredients; mix well. Pour over roast in Dutch oven and bring to a boil. Reduce heat, cover, and simmer for about two and a half hours, or until roast is fork tender. Set aside for about 15 minutes before slicing.

MEAT LOAF AND MUSHROOM GRAVY

2 lbs. ground beef
1 cup soft bread crumbs
1 egg
Salt and pepper to taste

Combine all the ingredients above; mix thoroughy. Shape mixture into a loaf to fit a standard-size loaf pan. Bake, uncovered, at 350 degrees for about an hour. Prepare mushroom gravy to serve over meatloaf.

Mushroom Gravy: In saucepan, melt two tablespoons butter. Add two cups sliced mushrooms and about half of an onion, finely chopped; cook over mediun heat until tender. Add two cups beef broth (canned), and simmer for about five minutes. Add two tablespoons corn starch to four tablespoons cold water; stir well and add to mushroom mixture. Cook for about a minute, until the gravy thickens. Serve it with meatloaf and mashed potatoes.

BEST BEEF STEW

1-1/2 lbs. stew meat, par-boiled
1 can cream of mushroom soup
1-1/4 cups Burgundy wine
1 pkg. dry onion soup mix

For sauce, mix together everything but the stew meat. Place meat in a baking dish and pour sauce over it. Bake at 300 degrees, uncovered, for about an hour and a half. Serves four. So easy and very tasty!

BEANS FOR BACKYARD BARBECUE

1 lb. bacon, cut in thirds
2 medium onions, chopped fine
5 cans pork and beans
1 bottle catsup
Brown sugar, 1 box (2-1/4 cups)
1/4 cup prepared mustard
1/4 cup Worcestershire sauce
2 teasp. Liquid Smoke

Fry bacon in big pan until crisp. Add onions, sauté until transparent, then add beans and stir. Add remaining ingredients; stir well and lower heat to simmer. Simmer uncovered until cooked to consistency, about two hours. Serves 20.

CORN CASSEROLE

2 cans cream style corn
1/2 cup corn meal
2 eggs
6 tabsp. vegetable oil
1 teasp. garlic salt
3 Jalapeno peppers, chopped
1/2 onion, chopped

Mix all ingredients and pour into greased casserole dish. Bake at 350 degrees about 40 minutes. Cover with grated cheese and bake until melted. Serves 8.

BAKED ONIONS

12 med. onions, thinly sliced
1 bag potato chips (3-3/4 oz.)
1/2 lb. med. Cheddar cheese
2 cans cream of mushroom soup
1/2 cup milk
1/8 teasp. red pepper (cayenne)

Place alternate layers of onions, crushed potato chips, and grated cheese in an oblong casserole dish. Pour mushroom soup and milk, mixed, over top of onion mixture. Sprinkle cayenne pepper over top and bake at 350 for about an hour.

CHOCOLATE SOUR CREAM POUND CAKE

1 cup butter, softened
2 cups sugar
1 cup brown sugar, packed
6 large eggs, or 7 medium
2-1/2 cups all purpose flour
1/4 teasp. baking soda
1/2 cup cocoa
1 carton sour cream (8 oz.)
2 teasp. vanilla extract

Beat butter at medium speed until soft and creamy, about two minutes. Gradually add sugars, beating at med. speed 5 to 7 minutes. Add eggs one at a time, beating until yellow cannot be seen.

Combine flour, baking soda, and cocoa, then add to creamed mixture alternately, with sour cream. Begin and end with flour mixture; mix at low speed just until blended. Add vanilla. Spoon batter into a greased and floured 10-inch tube pan, then bake at 325 degrees for one hour and 20 minutes. It's done if a wooden pick inserted in center comes out clean. Cool in pan on wire rack 15 minutes; remove from pan, cool completely.

EASY AMBROSIA

1 can (20 oz.) pineapple chunks, drained
1 can (11 oz.) Mandarin oranges, drained
1-1/2 cup seedless grapes
1 cup flaked coconut
1 cup miniature marshmallows
1/2 cup chopped pecans
1 tabsp. sugar
3/4 cup vanilla yogurt

Combine all ingredients in a large bowl. Chill for several hours, or serve immediately. Serves 8.

LUSCIOUS LEMON BARS

1 box yellow cake mix, with pudding
2 eggs
1/3 cup vegetable oil
1 pkg. cream cheese (8 oz.)
1/3 cup sugar
1 teasp. lemon juice, fresh

Mix cake mix, one of the eggs, and oil until crumbly. Set aside one cup of mixture, then pat remaining mixture into an ungreased cake pan, 13 x 9. Bake at 350 degrees for 15 minutes. Beat cheese, sugar, lemon juice and remaining egg until smooth. Spread over baked layer, then sprinkle with cup of mixture previously set aside. Bake 15 minutes more. Cool, then cut into bars.

Just outside of Tupelo, the Natchez Trace Parkway Visitors Center offers a quiet respite and Trace artifacts, and the Tupelo Artist Guild Gallery exhibits local and regional art. The City Museum features Elvis memorabilia, but the best place for Elvis lore is the Birthplace Center, which includes the house, a park, museum, memorial chapel, and a good gift shop.

Grenada

This town is not exactly in the Delta, but close; not exactly in the heart of Mississippi, but close. The best geographic description for Grenada is that it is in the Hill Country. Grenada is a clean and green town that's home to the state's largest lake, the 36,000 acre Grenada Lake boasting 148 miles of shoreline. See the pretty lake and learn more about the town at the Grenada Lake Visitors Center Musem, which overlooks the lake. You're likely to hear the story of how the town was founded. Here's what we heard...

Back in the early 1830s, there were two towns in close proximity, Tullahoma and Pittsburg. Both towns were developed by men who owned competing land companies, who happened to be arch rivals. So pronounced was their rivalry that they each operated ferries across the Yalobusha River, one from each settlement. In 1836, representatives of the two towns met to discuss ending the animosity and getting on with growth and development of the region. So on July 4 of that year, they had a marriage ceremony, of sorts, which resulted in the union of the two towns and a new name: Grenada.

Today, along with the excellent boating, camping, and fishing on Grenada Lake, there's a historic town offering great shopping and good restaurants, festivals --the largest being the big Thunder on the Water-- a safe-boating event that's held each June and draws more than 130,000 people. Quilters will be there in October for the annual Gore Springs Quilt Show, where antique quilts are side-by-side with colorful new ones.

Rumor has it that good food is to be found in Grenada, too. See below a few of the things you may be served as a guest in this town, and thankfully, the recipes are easy.

PECANS AND BRIE

2 tabsp. butter
1/3 cup brown sugar, packed
Wedge of Brie cheese, about .5 lb.
1/2 cup pecans
Dash cinnamon
Crackers

Remove skin from top of Brie. In skillet, melt butter and add brown sugar. Stir to melt and add pecans and cinnamon. Place Brie in pan suitable for broiling and spoon melted mixture over it. Broil for several minutes; carefully avoiding burning. Serve immediately with crackers. Serves 4.

SHRIMP DIP

1 cup salad-size shrimp, cooked
1 green onion, diced
Cream cheese, 8 oz.

Mix ingredients and place in small baking dish. Bake at 350 degrees for about 20 minutes. Serve with crackers or chilled vegetables.

TORTILLA SOUP

1/2 lb. lean ground beef or turkey
1 clove garlic, minced
1 onion, finely chopped
1 pkg. enchilada sauce seasoning
Chili powder, salt, to taste
1 can (1 lb.) crushed tomatoes
1 can (15-oz.) pinto beans, drained
1 can (15-oz.) black beans, drained
1 can (15-oz.) corn, drained
2 cups water
2 cups crushed tortilla chips

Brown meat with garlic and onion; place in soup pot. Add enchilada seasoning and mix well. Add remaining ingredients and bring to a boil. Reduce and simmer until ready to serve. Before serving, top each bowl of soup with grated cheese, a dollop of sour cream, and diced green onion. Easy and robust! If a thinner soup is desired, add more water.

BROCCOLI AND MUSHROOM CASSEROLE

1 lb. frozen broccoli flowerets, thawed
1 green onion, chopped
1 cup mushrooms, sliced
1 can cream of mushroom soup
1/2 cup mayonnaise
2 cups croutons
1 cup cheese, grated

Preheat oven to 450 degrees. Mix all ingredients; place into a 9x13 inch baking dish. Bake for 15 minutes. Serves 6.

ALMOND ASPARAGUS

1 bunch fresh asparagus
Scant 1-1/2 tabsp. vegetable oil
1/4 cup sliced almonds
1/4 cup water
1 teasp. sugar
1/4 teasp. salt
Pepper to taste
1/2 lemon

Wash and cut asparagus into thirds. Sauté almonds in one teaspoon oil for about one minute, high heat. Place remaining oil in skillet with asparagus, water, sugar, salt and pepper. Stir constantly for one minute, high heat. Lower heat, cover, cook for about 3 minutes, or until asparagus is tender. Squeeze lemon over asparagus, place on serving plate, top with almonds. Serves up to 4.

SMOKED DOVES

Marinate 10 to 20 dove breasts in this mixture for at least two hours:

1/4 cup lemon juice
1/2 cup Teriyaki sauce
1/2 cup semi-sweet red wine
1/4 cup melted butter
Salt and pepper to taste

After marinating, place in a smoker with mesquite wood, then smoke for 25 minutes. Do not overcook for dove breasts will get too dry. Serve on wild rice (or Cajun rice) with hot biscuits.

ITALIAN CHICKEN

4 boneless chicken breasts
1 jar (14 oz.) marinara sauce (or spaghetti sauce)
6 fresh basil leaves, finely chopped
1/2 cup grated Parmesan cheese
1/2 cup grated Mozzarella cheese

Cook chicken in a covered skillet over medium heat. Add a bit of water so that chicken does not burn; cook for about 5 minutes. While chicken is cooking, combine remaining ingredients in a bowl. When chicken is done, pour sauce over it, then cover and reduce heat to low. Simmer about 5 minutes, until cheese is melted. Serve over pasta; serves 4.

YOGURT PIE

1 container (8-oz.) peach yogurt (may use strawberry or other flavor)
1 small container frozen whipped topping, thawed
1 prepared Graham cracker crust

Fold yogurt into whipped topping and pour into crust. Freeze for about an hour before serving. To enhance, place fresh fruit slices over pie before serving.

ICE CREAM DE MENTHE

4 brownies or chocolate pound cake
4 scoops vanilla ice cream
4 tabsp. Creme de Menthe
4 tabsp. chocolate sauce

Place a brownie, chocolate pound cake, or chewy chocolate cookies on each dessert plate. Top with a scoop of ice cream and drizzle with Creme de Menthe and chocolate sauce.

The Golden Triangle

Columbus, Starkville, and **West Point** make up the region in northeast Mississippi known as the Golden Triangle. The towns of Aberdeen and Amory are in the vicinity, too, though not in the Triangle. The two latter towns, along with Columbus, are situated on the Tennessee-Tombigbee Waterway.

Columbus

Columbus is the biggest of the Golden Triangle cities, with a portion of its population owed to Mississippi University for Women --the W-- and the Columbus Air Force Base, a U.S. Air Force pilot training facility, one of the three left in the country. Both the W and the base provide an up-market ambiance for this old river city. The town is known for its amazingly preserved antebellum architecture, which includes marvelous old mansions left intact because Columbus was never invaded by Union forces during the Civil War. When Union General W.T. Sherman made his fiery march through the South during the war, he somehow bypassed Columbus, though other towns did not fare as well.

Today, Columbus hosts an annual tour of homes --The Pilgrimage-- a tour event that presents a great opportunity to see living history at its best. The unique thing about the Columbus Pilgrimage, as opposed to others in the South, is that these homes are lived in. They are not stiff and stuffy house museums; rather, they are appreciated and cared for by people who call them home. See more about "Pilgrimage" in the Mississippiana

Shadowlawn, Columbus.

section. In the meantime, the Columbus Welcome Center has information on homes open daily. They also have for sale a beautifully designed coffee table book that features the homes and history of Columbus, called "REFLECTIONS." The oustanding color photography shows why people come off the beaten path to see this pretty, historic town.

The nation's first Memorial Day took place in Columbus back in 1866, though at the time it was called Confederate Decoration Day. See more about Decoration Day *cum* Memorial Day in the "Mississippiana" chapter near the back of the book.

Columbus's most famous native son is the playwright Tennessee Williams, who won Pulitzer Prizes for *A Streetcar Named Desire, Cat on a Hot Tin Roof,* and critical acclaim for such theatre and film favorites as *The Glass Menagerie, Night of the Iguana,* and more. Tennessee, actually named Thomas Lanier Williams, was the grandson of The Rev. Walter Dakin, rector of St. Paul's Episcopal Church. The young Williams' family lived with the Dakins when young Tom was born, so the rectory was the first home of Tennessee Williams. Today, the gray and yellow Victorian rectory was moved a block from its former site on College Street to the corner of Main and Third, where it now serves as the official welcome center for the city.

Downtown Columbus has been updated and refurbished because of a renewed interest in downtown development and Main Street Mississippi, but the charm of earlier days is still very much intact. Part of Columbus's uniqueness has to do with the blending of the old and new, and the sophistication that filters down from the university and the well-traveled military people who choose to make their home here.

Columbus is a town of great cooks, and a great cookbook was published here in the 1980s, with most of the recipes provided by local culinary talent. The cookbook, currently out of print, is called *A Grand Heritage,* and indeed it is grand. Some of the recipes found in this section are from *A Grand Heritage*. Thanks to great chef and cookbook editor Juliaette Sharp for sharing the recipes from Grand Heritage, and for helping to proof this book, along with Jean Wilder and Carolyn Denton.

MISSISSIPPI CURRY DIP

1 garlic clove, minced
1 cup mayonnaise
1 tabsp. chili sauce
1 heaping tabsp. chutney (cut fine)
1 tabsp. Worcestershire sauce
2 tabsp. grated onion
1-1/2 teasp. curry powder
Pinch of salt
1 teasp. Louisiana hot sauce

Mix all ingredients. Serve with raw vegetables or shrimp.

GINNY'S ANTIPASTO

1 (14 oz.) can artichoke hearts
1 (3 oz.) can mushroom pieces
1 (10 oz.) jar salad olives, chopped
1 bottle Italian dressing

Layer coarsely chopped artichoke hearts, mushrooms, and olives. Pour salad dressing over this, seal and refrigerate. Make eight hours before serving. Serve with crackers. This will keep two weeks in refrigerator.

SALMON LOG

1 (1 lb.) can salmon
1 (8 oz.) pkg. cream cheese
1 tabsp. lemon juice
2 teasp. grated onion
1 teasp. prepared horseradish
1/4 teasp. salt
1/4 teasp. Liquid Smoke
1/2 cup chopped pecans
3 tabsp. snipped parsley

Combine salmon with next six ingredients; mix thoroughly. Chill several hours. Shape mixture into a 8 x 2 inch log. Combine pecans and parsley; roll salmon log in mixture. Chill well. Serve with assorted crackers. Serves 12.

CHICKEN SUPREME

12 chicken breast halves
2 cups dairy sour cream
1/4 cup lemon juice
4 teasp. Worcestershire sauce
1 teasp. celery salt
2 teasp. paprika
4 cloves garlic
4 teaspoons salt
1/2 teaspoons pepper
1-3/4 cups bread crumbs
1 cup butter, melted
1/3 cup parsley, chopped

Bone and skin chicken breasts. Combine next eight ingredients. Marinate the breasts overnight in the sour cream mixture. Remove and roll in bread crumbs. Pour one-half cup of melted butter over the breasts; bake in large oblong baking dish for 30 minutes at 325 degrees. Pour remaining half cup of butter over the breasts; cook another 30 minutes. Sprinkle with parsley and serve; serves 12.

STEAK AU POIVRE

1/4 cup fresh peppercorns
4 New York strip steaks
2 to 3 tabsp. oil
3 tabsp. butter
1/4 cup cognac
1/2 cup heavy cream
Salt and pepper to taste

Crush peppercorns and coat both sides of steak. Cover the bottom of sauté pan with oil and heat. Completely trim steaks, then sauté over medium to high heat. Remove steaks from pan and discard oil; add butter to the pan and return the steaks. Add cognac and ignite; allow to cook until flames cease. Remove steaks to serving platter and keep warm. Add cream to pan and stir with a wooden spoon over medium to high heat, so that cream will reach boiling point and thicken. Add one teaspoon cognac and salt & pepper to taste. Pour sauce over steak and serve immediately.

SHRIMP AND MUSHROOMS AU GRATIN

1/4 lb. fresh mushrooms, sliced
2 tabsp. butter
2 cups shrimp, boiled & peeled
3 tabsp. butter
4 tabsp. plain flour
1/2 teasp. dry mustard
1/4 teasp. each salt and pepper
1/2 teasp. Louisiana hot sauce
1 teasp. dried minced onion flakes
3/4 cup milk
1/2 cup white wine
1/4 cup grated Parmesan cheese
3/4 cup shredded Cheddar cheese
6 crackers, crushed

Sauté mushrooms in 2 tabsp. butter; add shrimp and mix well. Pour into greased casserole. Make sauce by melting 3 tabsp. butter in medium saucepan and blending in flour, mustard, salt, pepper, hot sauce, onion flakes, and milk. Cook over medium heat, stirring constantly until sauce thickens. Add wine slowly. Continue stirring and add the Parmesan and 1/2 cup Cheddar. When cheese is melted, pour over shrimp and mushrooms. Top with cracker crumbs and remaining cheese. In preheated oven, bake uncovered at 350 degree oven for 30 minutes. Serves 4.

SPINACH MADELINE

2 (10 oz.) pkgs. frozen, chopped spinach
4 tabsp. margarine
2 tabsp. plain flour
2 tabsp. chopped onion
1/2 cup evaporated milk
1/2 teasp. salt
1/2 cup vegetable liquid
3/4 teasp. celery salt
3/4 teasp. garlic powder
1 (6 oz.) roll jalapeno cheese
1 teasp. Worcestershire sauce

Cook and drain spinach, reserving the liquid. Melt margarine; add flour, stirring until smooth. Add onion; cook until soft, then add vegetable liquid and evaporated milk and cook until thick. Stir in seasonings and cut-up cheese; add spinach and put in cassesrole. Top with bread crumbs. Cook at 350 degrees until hot. Serves 6.

MISS GEORGIA'S ASPARAGUS LOAF

2 tabsp. butter
2 tabsp. flour
4 eggs
1 scant tabsp. gelatin
1 scant tabsp. lemon juice
Seasoning (salt, pepper, paprika)
1 can asparagus
1/2 pint whipped cream

Heat butter in double boiler. Strain flour (dissolved in water) into batter, stirring until it becomes thick; add beaten eggs and cook until done. Remove from fire, add dissolved gelatin. Add seasoning, lemon juice, etc. When cool add whipped cream. Line pan or mold with a half of the asparagus and pour over half of the mixture. Add another layer of asparagus and remaining mixture. Put in refrigerator until congealed.

MISS GEORGIA'S SAUCE FOR ASPARAGUS

1 cup sweet milk
3 tabsp. melted butter
3 egg whites
2 egg yolks
Salt to taste

Mix milk with melted butter and flour; add beaten egg yolks. Place in sauce pan and cook until thick as cream sauce. Beat egg whites stiff, then fold into sauce.

POTATOES ROMANOFF

6 large potatoes
1 pint dairy sour cream
1 bunch green onions, chopped
1-1/2 cup shredded Cheddar cheese
1-1/2 teasp. salt
1/4 teasp. pepper
Sprinkle of paprika

Boil potatoes in jackets; cool completely. Peel and shred potatoes; mix with other ingredients except paprika. Bake at 375 degrees for 30 minutes. Serves 12. NOTE: May prepare and refrigerate day before; bake before serving.

TOMATO-CHEESE PIE

1 (9-inch) pie crust
3 ripe tomatoes, peeled
Salt and pepper to taste
1 teasp. sweet basil
2 tabsp. chopped green onions
1 cup mayonnaise
1 cup shredded Cheddar cheese

Bake and cool pie crust. Fill crust with thick slices of ripe tomatoes. Combine remaining ingredients. Spread over tomatoes. Bake at 350 degrees for 30 minutes; serve immediately. Serves 4 to 6.

CAKE DELIGHT

1 box butter cake mix
1 (16 oz.) can Mandarin orange slices
4 eggs
1/2 cup vegetable oil

Grease and flour two 9-inch cake pans. Preheat oven to 325 degrees. Mix all ingredients (do not drain oranges); beat on medium speed for two minutes. Bake for 25 to 30 minutes. Cool completely before frosting.

ICING FOR CAKE DELIGHT

1 large can crushed pineapple
1 (3-3/4 oz.) package instant vanilla pudding
1 (9 oz.) can whipped topping, thawed

Sprinkle pudding mix over undrained pineapple; allow to set about five minutes; stir well. Fold in whipped topping. Ice cake layers, top and sides. Keep refrigerated.

PEACH CREAM PIE

1 cup sugar
5 tabsp. flour
1 cup sour cream
2 cups fresh, sliced peaches
1 (9-inch) unbaked pie shell
Pastry strips
1/4 teasp. salt
2 tabsp. sugar
1/4 teasp. cinnamon

Add sugar and flour to sour cream; mix peaches into cream mixture; pour into pie crust; place pastry strips over filling. Combine salt, sugar and cinnamon, sprinkle over top of pie. Bake at 400 degrees for 45 minutes.

LOUISIANA BREAD PUDDING

9 slices stale white bread
1-1/4 cups sugar
1 (13 oz.) can evaporated milk
4 egg yolks
1/3 cup melted butter
1 teasp. vanilla
2 cups milk
4 egg whites

Break bread into small pieces. Place in mixing bowl with one cup sugar, evaporated milk, 2 cups milk, vanilla, egg yolks, and melted butter. Mix well; pour into 10x8 baking pan. Bake in preheated 325 degree oven for 45 minutes. Remove from oven; make meringue. **Meringue:** Beat egg whites with 1/4 cup sugar until stiff. Cover pudding with meringue and rebake for 3 to 4 minutes, or until golden. May be served with rum sauce, see below.

Rum Sauce: 1 can evaporated milk, 1 cup fresh milk, 1 cup sugar, 1-1/2 tablespoons cornstarch, 3 tablespoons butter, 2 ounces rum. In double boiler, put milk, sugar and butter. When hot, dissolve cornstarch in a little water and add hot milk. Stir until thick. Remove from fire and add rum. Serves 12.

Talk of food in Columbus must include a great story that happens to be true. It is about the traditional Eighth of May Luncheon that has been an event at St. Paul's Episcopal Church since May 8, 1865. Though the Emancipation Proclamation had been signed by President Abraham Lincoln long before that date, it wasn't until May 8 that word reached Columbus. The story that's been told and re-told is that when the household servants heard about emancipation, they left the kitchens and went out to celebrate. Some of the women didn't know how to cook, so they met at the church to decide what to feed their families. Chicken salad would be good and relatively simple, they thought, so they prepared a special chicken salad that proved to be most delicious. Thus began the tradition of the locally pronounced "Ada May" luncheon at St. Paul's.

Every year, the Women of the Church have used this annual event as a fundraiser for their projects, and now, it is so popular that long lines form to be seated and to take-out the special chicken salad plate. In recent years, barbecue has been added, but the draw is the special chicken salad. Until recently, the recipe for the chicken salad was a carefully guarded secret. The recipe follows...

ST. PAUL'S EIGHT O' MAY LUNCHEON CHICKEN SALAD

Cooked Dressing

6 egg yolks
1/2 cup salad oil
1 teasp. dry mustard
1-1/2 tabsp. sugar
1 teasp. salt
Dash red pepper
1 tabsp. Worcestershire sauce
1/2 cup milk
1/2 cup vinegar

Salad:

6 cups cubed chicken
2 cups diced celery
Juice of 1 lemon
Salt, pepper, paprika, red pepper
1/2 cup mayonnaise
1 cup cooked dressing

Dressing: Beat egg yolks until lemon yellow; gradually add salad oil; add mustard, sugar, salt, red pepper and Worcestershire. Place in top of a double boiler over medium heat; stir in milk. Warm vinegar and add to egg mixture. Cook slowly and stir constantly until mixture is as thick as boiled custard.

Salad: For best results, boil one (5 to 7 lb.) hen until meat falls from thighs of chicken. While the meat is still warm, remove from bone and carefully remove all skin, gristle, veins, and small bones. Immediately cut into cubes. Pour lemon juice over diced celery and refrigerate several hours or overnight. Toss lemon and celery and mix with chicken, seasoning to taste with salt, pepper, paprika, and red pepper. Add mayonnaise and one cup cooked dressing to chicken mixture; mix well. Serves 6 to 8.

Starkville

Still in the Golden Triangle, Starkville boasts the big Mississippi State University, and come football season, tailgate parties are as festive as you'll find anywhere. Other Starkville attributes include exhibits and displays at MSU, as well as art galleries, and the Templeton Music Museum. One of Starkville's most interesting things to do is tour the A.B. McKay Food and Enology Lab at MSU. Trace the beginnings of wine, from grape growth to processing to storage in a wine cellar. If you're interested in becoming a wine connoisseur, this is the place to be, but by group appointment, please. Also at MSU, the new John Grisham Room honors the university's most famous alum.

There's something about Starkville that attracts residents. So often, graduates of MSU find a way to stay and become a permanent part of the community.

West Point

West Point is a quiet, lovely town that has a pretty park in the central business district. It's also the home of Bryan Foods and the golf club developed by George Bryan, the prestigious Old Waverly, said to be among the best in the country. Each Labor Day weekend, the population of West Point swells considerably when the 20,000 or so people come into town for the Prairie Arts Festival, complete with juried arts, crafts, entertainment, and so much more. Not far from West Point sits the nationally known Waverley Plantation, an outstanding Greek Revival mansion that is one of the state's most popular historic homes.

You may have seen Waverley on the A&E television program, America's Castles, or on the cover of a major magazine, but you can also see it on your own any day of the week. And whenever, however, you see Waverley, it will have been to your advantage, for this house is truly one of a kind.

Built in 1852, the grand mansion Waverley almost defies description, for it's hard to imagine the twin circular, cantilevered stairway that gracefully curves around three stories and supports balconies on each story. It is indeed a work of architectural art, with a 65-ft. span between the ground floor and the top of the cupola. From the foyer, looking up toward the cupola with 16 octagonal windows surrounding it, you wonder how these early craftsmen acquired the ingenuity to create this architectural art.

***Waverley is a Greek Revival**-style showplace that is listed on the National Register of Historic Places, it is a National Restoration Award winner, as well as being a National Historic Landmark, which is the most prestigious of honors. The home is a private residence that is open for daily tours; admission. The address is West Point, though Columbus claims it, too, for it is a Columbus Pilgrimage tour home. Columbus is known for its homes of history, and Waverley is one of many fine examples of antebellum architecture.*

HONEY BAKED HAM

1 cooked, bone-in ham (12-14 lbs.)
3 tabsp. whole cloves
1-1/2 cups light brown sugar, packed
2 tabsp. flour
2 tabsp. ea. honey and orange juice
2 tabsp. orange marmalade
1 tabsp. Dijon mustard
1 teasp. ea. cinnamon and nutmeg

Place ham, fat side up, in a rack in a large roasting pan. Score the fat into diamonds; stud with whole cloves. Pour about one inch of hot water into the pan and bake in 325 degree oven, uncovered, about two hours. To make the glaze, mix the remaining ingredients until smooth. After an hour and a half, remove ham from oven and gently remove the tough skin from the shank end. With a spatula, spread glaze over ham and continue baking 30 minutes longer, until the outside is browned and glazed. Cool 15 minutes before removing cloves and slicing.

REAL COUNTRY RIBS

2 racks (3-1/4 lbs.) country style pork spare ribs, trimmed
1-1/2 cups ketchup
3 tabsp. Worcestershire sauce
2 tabsp. brown sugar
2 tabsp. prepared mustard
Black pepper to taste
Pinch of red pepper

While grill or broiler is heating, place the ribs in a Dutch oven, add cold water to cover, and bring to boil. Lower heat and simmer for ten minutes, then place the ribs on paper towels to drain. Make sauce by combining remaining ingredients in small pan, then bring to a boil over moderate heat. Lower heat and simmer for about one minute.

Grill ribs over medium hot coals, or broil four inches from the heat for 15 minutes. Turn and baste with sauce several times.

HANNAH'S HAM LOAF

2-1/2 lbs. ground baked ham
1/2 lb. pork sausage
3 eggs, beaten
1 cup bread crumbs
1/4 teasp. pepper
1 cup milk
1 small can crushed pineapple
1-1/2 tabsp. prepared mustard
1/2 cup brown sugar

Grind ham in food processor (or have your butcher grind it). Mix the ham and sausage with eggs, bread crumbs, pepper, milk, and pineapple (save juice). Spread meat mixture in shallow baking dish. Mix mustard with brown sugar and spread over ham loaf. Bake about an hour and a half at 350 degrees. If ham loaf becomes dry, baste with reserved pineapple juice. Serves 8.

Note: May be served as a supper dish, on crackers as an appetizer, or in a sandwich.

SWEET POTATOES AND PINEAPPLE

2 cups cooked, mashed sweet potatoes
1 cup milk
1/2 cup pineapple juice
Marshmallows
1 cup diced pineapple
2 tabsp. butter
1/2 teasp. cinnamon

Mix all ingredients except marshmallows. Beat until light, adding more milk if necessary. Place in greased casserole in moderate oven and bake 30 minutes. Remove from oven, top with marshmallows, return to oven to brown. Serves 6.

EGGPLANT PARMESAN

1 (1-1/2 lb.) eggplant, peeled and sliced into 1/4-inch thick slices
1/2 cup grated Parmesan cheese
2 cups shredded part-skim mozzarella cheese
1-1/2 cups spaghetti sauce

Layer half of the eggplant, 1/4 cup Parmesan, 3/4 cup mozzarella, and half of spaghetti sauce in a two-quart baking dish (which has been coated with cooking spray). Repeat with remaining eggplant, Parmesan, spaghetti sauce, and 3/4 cup mozzarella. Bake at 350 degrees for about 35 minutes, then sprinkle with remaining 1/2 cup mozzarella cheese and bake five more minutes. Serves 6.

PEAS EPICUREAN

1 can green peas (English)
1 cup heavy cream
4 strips bacon
1/2 large onion, chopped
1 cup mushrooms, canned or fresh
1 tabsp. flour
Salt and pepper to taste
1 tabsp. Worcestershire sauce
Dash of seasoning salt
1/4 cup sherry

Chop uncooked bacon into pieces and sauté with onion until brown. If fresh mushrooms are used, sauté them at this time. Add flour and cream, stirring constantly over low flame. After sauce has thickened and is smooth, add seasonings, sherry and canned mushrooms. Add peas last and gently fold into mixture. Serves 8.

PUMPKIN CUSTARD PIE

- Old Recipe -

Crust: Combine 1-1/2 cups flour, 1/2 teasp. salt, 1/3 cup lard and 4 tabsp. water. Blend ingredients by hand and roll flat to cover 9-inch pie tin.

Filling:

1 cup cooked pumpkin
3 eggs
1 tabsp. flour
1/4 cup brown sugar
1/2 cup white sugar
1/2 teasp. salt
1/3 teasp. nutmeg
1/2 teasp. cinnamon
1 pint milk

Mix ingredients in order listed and pour into unbaked pie shell. Bake in 400 degree oven for about 45 minutes.

STRAWBERRY PARTY CAKE

1 small angel food cake
1/2 pkg. strawberry gelatine
1/2 cup boiling water
1/2 cup whipped cream
1 pkg. frozen berries or 1 cup sliced strawberries

Dissolve gelatin in boiling water. Cook until thick but not set. Add whipped cream and strawberries. Cut cake into three layers and spread filling between layers. Cover with additional whipped cream if desired and place in refrigerator several hours. Serves 6.

APPLE BUTTER PIE

- Old Recipe -

6 egg yolks
3 cups apple butter
3 tabsp. butter, melted
2 tabsp. flour, sifted
2 tabsp. light corn syrup
1 pint cream
1/2 cup sugar
1 teasp. cinnamon
1/2 teasp. nutmeg
1/2 pint whipping cream
2 (9-inch) pie shells

Beat egg yolks until thick. Add apple butter and stir in butter, sifted flour and syrup. Blend in cream and add sugar and spices. Pour into pie shells and bake 40 minutes at 375 degrees. When pies cool, top with whipped cream. Halve recipe for one pie.

The towns of Aberdeen and **Amory** are the kinds of places people who are looking for retirement sites love to know about. They're both small enough to know neighbors, and big enough to have certain amenities. Aberdeen is a town rich in architecture, where grand old homes and churches have given this town a sense of community since the early 1800s. The downtown area is still busy and active, too.

St. John's Episcopal Church, built in 1852, has a unique story. The bell sitting atop the pretty church is made of silver coin. It boasts an engraving that says it was presented to the church by A.D. Bowman and 35 New York merchants, in 1853. Apparently, there was a clergy connection, as in a New York clergyman who came South, then told his friends about the town and the church, though this is reliable speculation.

Amory boasts an event called "Stars Over Amory," which takes place every other year, and attracts Hollywood celebrities who come to entertain at a fundraiser for education. Amory native Sam Haskell, a vice president with the William Morris Agency in Beverly Hills, has professional ties with the entertainers who travel to Amory to raise money for a scholarship in honor of Haskell's mother. It's a well-organized gala, with the townspeople providing meals and lodging for the stars. Included on the marquee are Ann Margaret, Debbie Allen, Pam Tillis, Nell Carter, Diahann Carroll, Tom Arnold, Marilu Henner, Gary Collins, and others, including dignitaries such as England's Prince Edward. Two former "Miss Mississippi's," Mary Ann Mobley and Mary Donnelly Haskell, Sam's wife, can be found on stage, too.

From all accounts, the Hollywood people enjoy a taste of the South, and they are royally served up a sampling of Dixie cuisine. The Junior Auxiliary of Amory used the event to publish a cookbook called, "Look Who Came to Dinner," which features recipes used during the celebrity event. The first two recipes following are from that book.

CAJUN SHRIMP APPETIZER

4 quarts water
1 large onion, sliced
5 lbs. unpeeled shrimp
2 cups vegetable oil
1/4 cup hot sauce
1 teasp. olive oil
1 tabsp. minced garlic
1-1/2 tabsp. salt
1-1/2 tabsp. seafood seasoning
1-1/2 teasp. dried whole basil
1-1/2 teasp. dried whole oregano
1-1/2 teasp. dried whole parsley

Bring water and onion to a boil; add shrimp, cook for 3 to 5 minutes. Drain well; rinse in cold water; place in large bowl. Combine remaining ingredients and beat with a wire whisk, then pour over shrimp and toss. Cover; chill 8 hours. To serve, drain shrimp, then place in a lettuce-lined serving bowl. Serves about 25.

HAM ROLLS

1 can crescent rolls
1/2 lb. thin-sliced ham
Sesame seed
1 pkg. mozzarella cheese slices
Prepared mustard

Divide crescent rolls into four rectangles (press seams together). Spread with mustard. Top with one slice ham, one slice cheese. Cut each roll into six slices and bake at 350 until brown. Serves about 24.

GREAT GRITS ROMA

1 lb. hot bulk pork sausage
1-1/2 lbs. lean ground beef
3/4 cup regular grits
1 (14 oz.) jar pizza sauce
Salt and pepper to taste
1/4 teasp. garlic powder
1 large green pepper, chopped
1 medium onion, chopped
2-1/2 cups Cheddar cheese, shredded

Brown meats together in a large skillet, stirring until meat crumbles. Drain well. Cook grits according to package directions, then spoon into a lightly greasted 13x9 baking dish. Combine pizza sauce and next three ingredients. Layer half each of pizza sauce, meat, green pepper, onion, and cheese over grits. Repeat layers, omitting remaining cheese. Cover and bake at 325 degrees for 25 minutes. Add remaining cheese; bake, uncovered, five minutes longer. Serves 8.

GREEN BEANS AMANDINE

1/2 cup sliced almonds
2 lbs. fresh green beans
1/3 cup butter or margarine
1 tabsp. lemon juice
1 teasp. salt
1/4 teasp. pepper

Bake (350 degrees) almonds in a shallow pan about 8 minutes, or until toasted. Set almonds aside. Split beans lengthwise; cook in boiling water to cover for about 4 minutes or until tender; drain. Melt butter in large pan, add almonds, beans, lemon juice, salt and pepper, tossing to coat well. Serves 8.

Nearby **Macon** has a rich history, for it's in the heart of the rich prairie land where cotton ruled in the 1830s and 1840s. The prolific writer Ben Ames Williams was born in Macon in 1889. He wrote such classic American novels as *House Divided, The Strange Woman, Leave Her to Heaven,* and 29 other books. Among his relatives were Confederate officers in the Civil War, an association that he features in his books.

The clock tower at Mississippi University for Women.

Downtown Jackson on a quiet Sunday morning.

Geese, across from Broadmoor Baptist Church, Madison.

Chapter 5
The Capital City and Central Mississippi

Jackson

Jackson justifiably evokes pride in native Mississippians. Not only as the state capital, but as an irrepressible town that was called "Chimneyville" during the Civil War, when it was burned beyond recognition with only a few chimneys left standing. But Jackson re-invented itself, stronger and better than before, and look at its accomplishments today. No wonder people who live in Jackson don't want to consider moving away. It's a place of the heart for them.

The best place to get to know Jackson is in the hallowed halls of the old capitol building. It's a place where reverence prevails, and well it should, for much of Jackson and Mississippi's history took place here. This grand Greek Revival structure served as the state capitol from 1839 until 1903, and now it serves us well as the Mississippi State Historical Museum, known by most as The Old Capitol Museum.

Permanent and traveling exhibits keep the museum interesting, informative, and educational. The nation's first Civil Rights exhibit is housed here, as well as an exhibit depicting the lives and work of early Mississippi women.

Mississippi artists are well represented at the Mississippi Museum of Art, which boasts the world's largest collection of work by Mississippi artists, and that's as it should be. Traveling exhibits often have an international scope.

Once you get around the unwieldy name, there's no better place to see the best of Mississippi than at the Jim Buck Ross Mississippi Agriculture and Forestry/National Aviation Museum. Can you imagine a school child trying to remember that moniker? Europe has a good idea: honor men of distinction with statues rather than naming public places for them. Locals call it the Ag Museum, and it is an outstanding living history museum that includes a 1920s-era farm, a turn-of- the century small town, and a big exhibit building where crop duster airplanes and other elements of the state's agricultural heritage are proudly exhibited. The 40-acre Ag Museum also includes a Heritage Center, a crafts gallery and a restaurant. An added bonus is the rose garden, which is fine enough to be listed on the National Rose Register.

Also on the grounds of the Ag Museum is the Mississippi Music Hall of Fame. The exhibit honors the state's contribution to the world of music, which includes a most impressive list: Elvis Presley, B.B. King, Tammy Wynette, Conway Twitty, the Blackwood Brothers, Faith Hill, Robert Johnson, Muddy Waters, Charley Pride, and opera diva Leontyne Price, among many.

Nearby, the Mississippi Sports Hall of Fame and Museum honors the state's sports heroes, and they are legion. Past and present champions live forever in rare archival footage --more than 850 interviews and information. This facility is futuristic, with touch-screen kiosks, and interactive technology which allows visitors to actually tee up and play legendary golf courses.

International ballet comes to Jackson every fourth year, and the beneficiaries are the ballet dancers who have a chance to perform and compete in this prestigious event, and those lucky enough to see it. In 1982, through a joint resolution of the U.S. Congress, Jackson was designated the official home of the USA International Ballet Competition. The IBC has been called the "Olympics of Dance," since competitors vie for gold, silver and bronze medals, as well as cash and scholarships.

Other world-wide host cities are Moscow, Helsinki, Paris, and Varna (Bulgaria). The competition is rotated among these cities. The rotation was in Jackson in 1998. Jackson is also the residence for the professional companies, the Ballet Mississippi and Ballet Magnificat. The latter is the only Christian ballet company in the United States.

Jackson is surely a special place, for it is the city that nurtured the creative writing talents of Miss Eudora Welty. The acclaimed photographer and author was born in Jackson in 1909, and even though she ventured away from time to time, she always came back home. Perhaps she chose to return to write about the familiar, for most of her fiction is set in Mississippi. The kind and gentle Miss Welty died in her beloved Jackson in July, 2001. She will be forever missed, but her work will live on as long as there are books.

She once said in an interview that Southern writers care profoundly about place, not in the philosophical or historical sense, but...*"in the worlds of sight and sound and smell, in its earth and water and sky and in its seasons."*

Miss Welty later said that Mississippians have a character that does not stem from sense of place or historical significance, and that it has nothing to do with living in the past. *"It's a sense of community that has always characterized us, I think: a knowledge of family stories, that sense of generations and continuity. That gives us an identity."*

Because of the writings of Eudora Welty, more of us have a stronger sense of what it's like to be Mississippians. She received the Pulitzer Prize for *The Optimist's Daughter.* Among the other beloved works are *The Ponder Heart* and *Delta Wedding*. Her short story, *The Worn Path*, is a national favorite.

Another great Mississippi writer has Jackson roots, and she is the late Margaret Walker Alexander. Her book, *Jubilee*, was a national bestseller. Today, the Margaret Walker Alexander National African-American Research Center examines life during the Civil War, segregation, and the Civil Rights years.

Mynelle Gardens is a colorful respite for Jacksonians and others who appreciate the beauty of nature. The city purchased the glorious seven-acre botanical park in 1973, long after Mrs. Mynelle Westbrook Hayward began planting and nurturing her garden. Something is in bloom year 'round at Mynelle Gardens.

Wherever you go in Jackson, from the many good restaurants to the homes of Jacksonians, you find the most terrific food. Great chefs reside here, and the fare ranges from very sophisticated Continental cuisine to down-home peas and cornbread. Whatever it is, you can count on it being well-prepared and tasty. Following is an overview of the kinds of food you're likely to find in Jackson and across central Mississippi...

SESAME BITES

1 loaf thin sandwich bread
1 (8 oz.) pkg. cream cheese, softened
2 tabsp. chopped chives
1/4 cup plus 2 tabsp. butter, melted
1/2 cup sesame seeds, toasted

Trim crust from bread, then use rolling pin to flatten each slice. Combine cream cheese and chives; mix well. Spread mixture evenly on flattened bread; roll up. Brush log with butter and roll in sesame seeds. Place seam side down on baking sheet. Cover and chill. Then, slice each log into three pieces. Bake at 350 degrees for about 15 minutes. Makes 5 dozen.

BRAISED PORK ROAST VIENNESE

1 (3 lb.) boneless pork loin roast
1/4 cup bacon drippings
1 cup chopped onion
1 cup chopped carrot
1 teasp. paprika
1 tabsp. snipped parsley
3/4 cup chicken broth
2 tabsp. all-purpose flour
1/2 cup dairy sour cream
1/4 teasp. caraway seed
1 teasp. chopped capers

In Dutch oven, brown roast in bacon drippings; set roast aside and cook onion and carrot until tender, but not too brown. Stir in paprika. Lay roast atop vegetables; add chicken broth. Bake, covered, in 350 degree over for about two hours, or until meat thermometer registers 170 degrees. Remove roast; keep warm. Strain pan drippings, discard vegetables. Measure pan drippings, skim off excess fat. Add water to drippings, if necessary, to measure 1-1/3 cups. Return to Dutch oven. Blend flour into sour cream; stir into liquid in pan. Cook and stir 'til thickened and bubbly. Stir in caraway seed, capers and parsley. Serve with roast. Serves 6.

BREAST OF CHICKEN WITH SAFFRON RICE

6 chicken breasts, split
1/3 cup butter
1/4 cup onion, finely chopped
1-1/2 quarts chicken broth
Salt and pepper to taste
2 cups rice
1 bay leaf
Few sprigs parsley
Thyme
Saffron

Season chicken with salt and pepper, then brown in butter, turning frequently. When browned, remove from skillet. Add to skillet the onion and brown; add rice and more butter if needed. Add a sprinkle of saffron; mix well. Add sprinkle of thyme, parsley and bay leaf. Cook for about five minutes, stirring often. In a Corningware dish, place the rice first, then arrange chicken over it and pour the chicken broth over all. Bring to a quick boil and cover tightly. Bake at 375 degrees for about 30 minutes, or until rice has absorbed chicken stock. Serve on a platter, with chicken over the mound of rice. Sprinkle with minced parsley. Serves 6.

ELEGANT AND EASY CRAB BISQUE

2 (7 oz.) cans crabmeat
2 cans tomato soup
1 can pea soup
2 cups heavy cream
2/3 cup dry sherry
Garnish: sour cream and chives

Flake crabmeat; heat with soups and cream, but do not boil. Stir in sherry; reheat. Garnish each serving with a tablespoon or so of sour cream, with chives sprinkled over sour cream. Serves 8.

SPINACH-ARTICHOKE CASSEROLE

1/2 cup onion, chopped
1/2 cup butter
2 (10 oz.) pkgs. frozen, chopped spinach thawed and drained
1 (14 oz.) can artichoke hearts (in water) drained, coarsely cut
1/2 cup grated Parmesan cheese
1 cup sour cream
1 (4 oz.) can mushroom pieces
1/4 teasp. red pepper
Salt to taste (taste first)

Sauté onion in butter. Combine remaining ingredients; add to sautéed onions. Bake in deep, covered casserole at 350 degrees for 25 minutes. Serves 6.
Note: May garnish with pimento strips, or finely chopped green onion, green part.

BROILED BABY ZUCCHINI WITH ROSEMARY

4 zucchini, halved lengthwise
1-1/2 tabsp. butter, melted
1/2 teasp. crumbled rosemary
1/4 teasp. salt
Pepper to taste
1 teasp. fresh lemon juice

In pre-heated broiler, brush the zucchini with melted butter and place, cut-side down, on a broiler pan lined with aluminum foil. Broil for about four minutes. Turn the zucchini, season with rosemary, salt and pepper to taste. Broil two to five minutes longer, until crisp and tender. Squeeze lemon juice over zucchini; serve hot. Serves 4.

POTATOES DRESSED IN CHEESE

10 or 12 new potatoes
1/2 cup melted butter
Salt and pepper to taste
I cup grated cheese
1/4 cup grated onion

Boil new (or red) potatoes, in jackets, until tender. Remove the skins and roll in melted butter, then roll in grated cheese seasoned with salt and pepper, and grated onion. Place in shallow buttered dish and bake at 400 degrees for about 10 or 15 minutes.

BLACKBERRIES 'N SHERRY

2 pints fresh blackberries
3 egg yolks
1 cup sugar
Dash of salt
2 tabsp. dry sherry
1 cup whipping cream

Put all ingredients --except berries and whipping cream-- in a double boiler. Bring to a boil and cook for ten minutes, stirring constantly. Refrigerate until cool; stir in a little more sherry to soften, if needed. Whip cream and fold into sherry mixture. Spoon over individual servings of blackberries in dessert bowl. Serves 6.

PRALINE ICE CREAM PIE

1/2 cup packed brown sugar
1/2 cup whipping cream
2 tabsp. butter
1 cup chopped pecans
1 teasp. vanilla
1-1/2 quarts vanilla ice cream
1 baked 9-inch pasty shell
3 egg whites
1/2 teasp. vanilla
1/4 teasp. cream of tartar
1/3 cup granulated sugar
Rum sauce (recipe follows)

In skillet, over medium-low heat, heat and stir brown sugar just until it melts, about 10 or 12 minutes. Gradually blend in cream and cook about 3 minutes more, until smooth. Remove from heat; stir in butter, pecans and 1 teasp. vanilla. Cool. Stir ice cream just to soften. Quickly fold in praline mixture, which has been cooling. Turn into pastry shell, then freeze. Just before serving, beat egg whites, 1/2 teaspoon vanilla, and the cream of tartar until soft peaks form. Gradually add sugar, beating to stiff peaks. Spread meringue over ice cream mixture, sealing to edge. Bake at 475 degrees for 4 or 5 minutes, or until lightly browned. Serve immediately with Rum Sauce. Serves 6 or 8.

Rum Sauce: In small saucepan, combine two beaten egg yolks, 1/2 teasp. grated lemon peel, 1/4 cup lemon juice, 1/4 cup sugar, and 4 tabsp. butter. Cook and stir til thickened. Stir in three tablespoons light rum. Makes about one cup.

EASY SUNSHINE CAKE

1 box yellow cake mix
1 box instant lemon pudding
4 eggs
3/4 cup water
3/4 cup oil

Mix all ingredients and bake in 9 x 13 pan as directed on box. When cake is done, while hot, prick with fork and pour glaze over the top, covering it entirely.
Glaze: 1/3 cup orange juice, 2 cups sifted powdered sugar, 2 teasp. vanilla.

And then there's Canton, where the pre-Civil War Madison County Courthouse serves as an anchor for the town. It's one of the few old Mississippi courthouses still intact and unaltered. Canton is a lovely place where the town square, laid out in 1833, is the focal point of activity. Union torches destroyed most of the original commercial buildings, though they were re-built in the 1880s. The homes fared better; many of them are recipients of stories of events that occurred during the Yankee invasion.

One event happened at the house now generally known as the A.K. Foote home, though at the time it was the residence of Dr. A.H. Cage and family. According to the story, when the Union Army captured Canton, they also took all the livestock. The Cages had a new baby who desperately needed milk from the confiscated cow. The brave Mrs. Cage paid a visit to the Union command post, demanding the return of her cow. Her mission was accomplished; a soldier was instructed by the commanding officer to return the cow to the Cage home, with the admonition: "M'aam, take good care of this cow and keep her close." She did, in her bedroom, for the remaining five days of the Yankee invasion of Canton.

Madison County Courthouse, Canton.

Twice a year, the town swells with thousands of people who come for the big Canton Flea Market each May and October, held on the Courthouse lawn and around downtown. This event attracts Mississippians and others from across the South.

Near Jackson, the Petrified Forest at **Flora** boasts the remains of giant trees that have been around about 36 million years. It is the only petrified forest in the eastern United States, and it is a National Natural Landmark. The Cactus Plantation at **Edwards** features more than 3500 varieties of the thorny cacti, bromeliads, daylilies, tropical foliage and seasonal plants.

Southeast of Jackson, the Piney Woods Country Life School is a testament to the dedication of a black educator who came to the region in the early 1900s with less than $2 to his name, and a Bible. Founded by Dr. Laurence Jones in 1909, the boarding school for disadvantaged African-American students is still going strong today. Dr. Jones's philosophy has proved to be so successful other schools have used it as a role model. His aim was to balance academic knowledge with vocational skills. So astute was his skill as an orator, he talked himself out of a lynching and got the would-be lynching mob to donate money to his cause, which was the Piney Woods Country Life School. Today the beautiful campus and museum welcomes visitors to tour the school and grounds, including five lakes and fertile farmland. Dr. Jones died at the age of 93 in 1975, but not before inspiring generations of educators and students. The school is about 20 miles south of Jackson on Highway 49, in the Piney Woods community.

Northeast of Jackson, this town had adverse publicity during the Civil Rights conflict, and certainly not all the people in the town subscribed to racist activities, but the reputation of racism lingered. Today, **Philadelphia** is a pretty town with friendly people who are pleased to invite visitors to the town's stellar events and activities, among them the Neshoba County Fair and the Choctaw Indian Fair, both annual summertime events, and both very popular.

One of Philadelphia's favorite sons was the highly respected journalist, Turner Catledge, who served as the long-time editor of *The New York Times.* Currently, native Philadelphian Dan Jordan, Ph.D, is the executive director of the Thomas Jefferson Foundation, which oversees the major piece of American history, Monticello, near Charlottesville, Virginia.

Everything pertaining to the Mississippi Band of Choctaw Indians began with Nanih Waiya, the legendary birthplace of the Choctaw. The Choctaws keep their traditions alive during the week-long fair each July, which includes the wearing of colorful costumes, dancing, native crafts, and the coronation of the Choctaw Princess. With the advent of a Las Vegas-style gaming casino, which is owned by the Choctaws, their fortunes have increased considerably. Along with the Silver Star Casino in Neshoba County, which includes the casino proper, a hotel, several restaurants, golf courses, and more, the Choctaws are now people who engage in big business.

Another big event in late July/early August is the Neshoba County Fair, often called Mississippi's Giant House Party because it is a camp-town fair, actually the only one left in the country. Families and friends gather in the camp houses to visit, eat, and have a grand old time. Camp 'houses' are passed down from generation to generation, and they are not readily available otherwise. Festival-goers are entertained by musicians, horse-races, harness racing, crafts, carnival rides, and so much more. The Fairgrounds is listed on the National Register of Historic Places. See more about "the Fair" in the Mississippiana section near the back of the book.

"How yawl?" That's what you're likely to hear often at the Neshoba County Fair, truly Mississippi's Giant House Party, and the place for state-wide politicians to stump and greet the week-long residents of the 475 cabins and the 85,000 or so day visitors. The fair began as a private agricultural fair in 1899, when caravans of wagons came to the fairgrounds to swap farm products and animals. Tents were pitched at first, then the cabins were constructed. Today, the rustic, tin-roof cabins are coveted possessions and much in demand as gathering places for family and friends to partake of great food, good times, and entertainment. In the 1970s and 80s, country stars performed regularly at the Fair, among them Loretta Lynn, Jerry Lee Lewis, and Barbara Mandrell. The fairgrounds are located seven miles southwest of Philadelphia on Highway 21 South.

Meridian

For a town that was burned by the Union Army and declared "...no longer existing," Meridian has shown us a thing or two about growth. The citizens apparently decided not to accept defeat, for they began to re-build with gusto. Trains, planes and highways have been a factor in that growth, thanks to aviation pioneers, the Key brothers, the Meridian Regional Airport, and the U.S. Naval Air Station -- and to the location of the town, which appealed to rail interests. Two interstate highways, I-20 and I-59 join at Meridian, so transportation-wise, it's a city in its prime.

Jimmy Rodgers, also known as "the Singing Brakeman" because of his early job with the railroad, is said to be the father of country music. In his honor, Meridian built the Jimmy Rodgers Museum, and the city hosts an annual Jimmy Rodgers Festival, which attracts country music wanna-be's from throughout the South.

Meridian's Grand Opera House (c. 1890) has in the past attracted such stars as Sarah Bernhardt and Helen Hayes. The Opera House, soon to be regally restored, came into being shortly before the Dentzel Carousel, made between 1892 and 1899 by Gustav Dentzel. It is thought to be the only two-row stationary Dentzel menagerie still in existence. Thus, it is a National Historic Landmark. Merrehope, the grand 20-room antebellum mansion, is open for tours Monday - Saturday.

The Peavey Visitors Center is not old, but it is most impressive. Peavey Electronics is the largest manufacturer of amplifiers, guitars and keyboards in the world, and they began in Meridian. Trace the history of the company through the musicians who used Peavey equipment. The Peavey Visitors Center and Museum is located on Marion Russell Road off Highway 45 Bypass.

Another site recognized by historians is the Causeyville General Store and gristmill, which opened in 1895. It's an actual general store, but it also has Mississippi gift items and it houses a music museum.

South of Meridian, you will be surprised to find a 65-foot waterfall and water park. It's Dunn's Falls on the Chunky River, and along with the beautiful scenery, there's a natural wildlife refuge and picnic area, as well as a hiking trail.

Causeyville General Store, Meridian.

Chapter 6
South Mississippi and the Gulf Coast

The South Mississippi region has its own personality. There's an independent spirit prevalent here, for the Piney Woods people made up their own minds a long time ago. During the Civil War, some of them wanted no part of a war that would serve the plantation system, for there were no plantations in these parts. Certain counties, among them Jones, Wayne, Jasper, Forrest, Smith, Covington, Perry, and Greene were more interested in timber than farming, so big farms were indeed scarce. The few big farms used sharecroppers, not slaves.

Here's an excerpt from a published history of Laurel and Jones County, written by the Women of St. Paul's Church, first edition printed more than one hundred years ago:

"The Civil War made little difference in the mode of life of these early inhabitants who lived in log houses, fashioned of peeled pine poles, with batten doors and windows, cooked on open fireplaces in clay and stick chimneys, used dried turkey breast for flour, made their own sugar, tanned their own leather in a big gum trough, raised their tobacco, spun three or four yards of homespun a day, dyed it and thus merited the title, 'copperas breeches,' manufactured their own soap, carved their plowstocks and made teeth for their harrows by whittling wooden pegs, built their wagons which they called 'tarpoles' because the poles were greased with tar. They hitched three or four yoke of oxen to each to drag it laboriously to Mobile and back, one hundred and twenty-five miles to the nearest market."

That pretty much capsulates the early lifestyle in South Mississippi. The people were independent-minded and entirely self-sufficient. With the arrival of the "lumber barons" in the late 1800s, the region lost most of its virgin timber and much of its identity. Men left the farms to work in the mills, and the culture of the region began to change. Where tall pines and hardwood once grew wild and free, mud holes and barren land took the place of the majestic trees. But once again, the resilient Piney Woodsmen and woodswomen went about the business of forging lives for themselves and their families.

Today, South Mississippi's culture is a little bit of pioneer spirit propelled by the Protestant work ethic, with certain attitudes borrowed from neighbors New Orleans and Mobile. If you lived in South Mississippi a few years back --before the advent of cable television-- you more than likely listened to New Orleans radio and read either or both the New Orleans Times Picayune or the Mobile Press Register. So the culture remains an interesting blend of country and city, sophistication and shyness, with new cultural influences now coming in from the African American population.

South Mississippi is still a place where people care about their neighbors, and they take the time to visit within their communities. It is a place where church attendance is a way of life, and where family reunions are much-anticipated events. It's a place one can easily call 'home.'

Laurel

Laurel, in Jones County, officially became a town in 1881, after the lumber industry and the railroads arrived on the scene and needed a town to hang their hats on. In the early 1900s, Laurel was called the lumber capital of the world, with yellow pine from the Piney Woods shipped to all points north.

And thanks to an accidental but innovative process developed in 1926 by William Mason, formerly of Iowa, wood waste was turned into a usable --and marketable-- product called Masonite. Shortly thereafter, Masonite Corporation in Laurel became the major supplier, world-wide, of the versatile hardboard. Luckily, about the time timber was depleted, oil was discovered in 1942, and Laurel soon became the oil center of Mississippi, with fertile oil fields in the nearby communities of Heidelberg, Eucutta, Soso, Pachuta, and Shubuta.

Laurel today is home to one of the prettiest streets in the state, the tree-canopied Fifth Avenue, and it is the home of the Lauren Rogers Museum of Art, by far one of the finest museums in the South. The Lauren Rogers, founded in 1923, was the first art museum in Mississippi, and it deserves the rave reviews bestowed upon it today. The impressive Georgian Revival-style building was designed by the architect Rathbone deBuys of New Orleans, with interiors done by the Chicago firm of Watson and Walton. Expect to find an outstanding collection of world-wide and native basketry, Japanese woodblock prints, a superb collection of Georgian silver, a permanent collection of paintings that include pieces by major American and European artists of the 19th and 20th centuries --among them Winslow Homer and Grandma Moses-- and an extensive reference library.

Lauren Rogers Museum of Art, Laurel.

The Lauren Rogers is so successful because of a coterie of dedicated docents, among them native Jones Countian Mary Jo Wedgeworth. Mary Jo is known to be a woman who gets things done, whether it's a project for the museum, her church, her local garden club, or a statewide garden club council, her talents do not go unnoticed. Mary Jo makes home life an art form, and does so effortlessly. In fact, she could write a "How-To" book and give Martha Stewart a run for her money.

As the only girl in a family of eleven children, the former Mary Jo Morgan learned her skills from her mother, then developed them more precisely through work with the 4-H Club and Home Demonstration Clubs at the local and statewide levels. Today, she lectures throughout the South on home-making, from planning party themes to preparing food, and her flower arrangements are legendary. She teaches a program on flower arranging and she is a master flower show judge. Mary Jo is also past president of the Garden Clubs of Mississippi.

Among Wedgeworth's honors: winner of the Governor's Initiative for Volunteer Excellence, and Outstanding Senior Citizen of the Year. It's people like Mary Jo who help keep Mississippi a special place. I say this with first-hand knowledge, because I've had the privilege of knowing her all my life. She was my Sunday School teacher. She shares a few of her recipes in the following section.

Landrum's Country Store and Homestead Village shows us the way things were in the early days, complete with a trading post, blacksmith shop, general store and more. The Landrum family has deep South Mississippi roots, so they've recreated the things that their ancestors may have been involved with. Their place is a few miles out from Laurel, on Highway 15 South.

Opera diva Leontyne Price hails from Laurel. As a young girl, her amazing talent was discovered by a local patron of the arts, who arranged for the young woman to study at Juilliard. Ms. Price maintains a Laurel connection, though she lives in New York City; she is retired from the Metropolitan Opera but conducts Master classes in voice.

Laurel boasts a plethora of good cooks from many of the surrounding communities as well as the town proper. One special occasion that's dear to my heart is "Ladies Day Out" each Tuesday at the fine old Laurel YWCA, organized in 1902. "Y" board members and volunteers serve the delicious luncheon to anyone who cares to attend. Some of the recipes below were taken from various old cookbooks put out by the "Y" in Laurel. A few choice recipes were taken from the very old "Laurel Cook Book," published by the Women of St. John's Guild (Episcopal), first printed in the year 1900. My prized copy is the fifth edition, revised and reprinted in 1949, given to me by the late Mrs. Billie Boone.

CRUNCHY PARTY CHEESE

1 (8 oz.) Edam or Gouda cheese round
2 oz. blue cheese or Roquefort
1 (3 oz.) pkg. cream cheese
1/8 teasp. nutmeg
2 tabsp. sour cream
1/4 cup toasted almond, chopped

Warm cheese at room temperature. Cut top off Edam or Gouda round; scoop out carefully, then mash cheese well. Crumble blue cheese and add to Edam or Gouda with cream cheese. Add nutmeg; blend thoroughly. Mix in two remaining ingredients. Place mixture back into scooped out shell. Serve with crackers or Melba toast rounds.

CLAM DIP

2 (3 oz.) pkgs. cream cheese
1 small can minced clams
Salt to taste, if needed
1 teasp. lemon juice
1 teasp. Worcestershire sauce
1/8 teasp. cayenne pepper

Mash cheese; drain clams and add clam juice to cheese until it is of dipping consistency. Add Worcestershire, onion juice, salt and pepper. Stir in minced clams; serve with party crackers.

CAVIAR MOUSSE

1 tabsp. unflavored gelatin
2 tabsp. cold water
1/2 cup hot water
1 tabsp. lemon juice
1 tabsp. Worcestershire sauce
2 tabsp. mayonnaise
1 pint sour cream
1 pinch dry mustard
4-1/2 ounces caviar

Soak gelatin in cold water until soft. Add boiling water, stir until dissolved. Add lemon juice and Worcestershire. In another bowl, combine mayonnaise and sour cream. Pour liquid mixture into this. Add pinch of dry mustard and caviar. Mix gently but thoroughly and pour into 3 or 4 cup mold. Chill six hours. Unmold by dipping the mold into hot water, and shaking contents loose onto serving plate. Garnish and serve as hors d'oeuvres or place in individual molds to serve as first course.

MARY JO'S CHICKEN BEARNAISE

2 cups cooked, chopped chicken breast
1 can cream of chicken soup
2 cups sour cream
1 pkg. Knorr Bearnaise Sauce Mix
1 small onion, finely chopped
Dash seasoning salt
Dash garlic salt (to taste)

Mix together and let set overnight. Bake at 250 degrees for 45 minutes. Serve over tri-colored noodles or put in puff pastry shells. Serves 8.

SCAMPI WITH PASTA

1 lb. shrimp, shelled and deveined
1 tabsp. salt
3 quarts boiling water
8 oz. pasta (spaghetti)
1/4 cup butter or margarine
Dash basil
3 tabsp. olive oil
2 cloves garlic, crushed
1/2 teasp. salt
1/2 teasp. oregano
1/2 cup chopped parsley
Grated Parmesan cheese

Cook pasta; drain. In skillet, melt butter; add oil, garlic, salt, oregano, basil. When hot, add shrimp and cook until pink. Serve over pasta; sprinkle with parsley and Parmesan. Serves 4.

STEAK FLAMBE`

4 (6 oz. pieces) sirloin steak, cut 1" thick
6 tabsp. butter
Salt and pepper to taste
1/4 cup brandy
1/2 cup whipping cream
3 tabsp. mustard (Dijon)
2 tabsp. dairy sour cream
1 teasp. Worcestershire sauce

Pound steak pieces to about 1/2-inch thickness. In large skillet, heat butter and saute steak for two or three minutes. Turn and sesason with salt and pepper. Cook to desired degree of doneness. Pour brandy over steaks; ignite. When flame dies, transfer steaks to warm serving platter.

To remaining juice in skillet, add whipping cream, mustard, sour cream and Worcestershire. Cook, stirring, until heated through. Pour sauce over steaks and serve. Serves 4.

TIMBALES OF FOWL

(Old "Laurel Cook Book" Recipe)

1 pint ground chicken or turkey
1 tabsp. butter
2 tabsp. bread crumbs
2 eggs
1/2 cup chicken stock
Salt and pepper to taste
1/2 onion, finely chopped

Melt butter and add bread crumbs, then add stock. When smooth, season. Add the chicken, and just before removing from fire, add eggs. Fill muffin pans with the mixture and place in a pan of hot water. Bake for 20 minutes, until firm but not brown. Carefully remove the timbales from the pans to a hot platter and serve with cream sauce.

CABBAGE BALLS

(Old "Laurel Cook Book" Recipe)

Boil cabbage until tender; chop rather fine, season, and form into small balls, about the size of walnuts. Roll balls in Parmesan or other grated cheese and bake until brown.

SWEET POTATO PONE

1 cup sugar
2 eggs
1 stick margarine
1 small can Pet milk
1/4 teasp. salt
Rind and juice of 1 orange
2 cups grated raw sweet potatoes
(cover with milk for coloration)

Mix above ingredients and bake in buttered casserole at 325 degrees for 45 minutes.

GREEN BEANS THE OLD WAY

4-6 slices bacon
1 large onion, chopped
2 lbs. green beans, snapped
1/2 cup water
Salt and pepper to taste
6-8 new potatoes
1/4 teasp. sugar

Fry the bacon in heavy pot until crisp; remove and drain. Add onion to bacon grease and sauté until wilted. Add green beans, water, salt and pepper, potatoes, and sugar. Cover and simmer for about 45 minutes or until tender. Place in serving dish; crumble bacon over top. Serves 6.

PINEAPPLE COCONUT PIE

9-inch pie shell, unbaked
3 eggs
1/4 cup sugar
1/4 teasp. salt
1 can (8 oz.) crushed pineapple
1 cup white corn syrup
1 cup flaked coconut
2 tabsp. melted butter
1 teasp. vanilla

Beat eggs; beat in sugar and salt. Stir in undrained pineapple, syrup, coconut, vanilla and butter. Pour into pie shell. Bake at 400 degrees for 45 minutes, or until center is set. Cool before cutting. Serve with a dollop of whipped cream.

OLD-FASHIONED POUND CAKE

1 lb. cake flour
1 teasp. baking powder
2 teasp. nutmeg
1 lb. butter (2 cups)
1 lb. sugar (2-1/4 cups)
1/4 cup lemon juice
1 lb. eggs, separated (10 eggs)

Mix flour, baking powder, and nutmeg. Sift three times. Cream butter until soft. Add sugar, gradually creaming until very fluffy. Add lemon juice and well-beaten egg yolks, beating very thoroughly. Fold in stiffly beaten egg whites, and then the flour. Turn into greased loaf pans covered with wax paper. Cook in slow oven, 325 degrees, for 1-1/4 to 1-1/2 hours. Makes two loaves.

FAVORITE CHOCOLATE CANDY

1 small can Pet milk
1-2/3 cups sugar
6 oz. pkg. chocolate chips
1-1/2 cups mini marshmallows

Mix and cook over low heat until bubbles begin to form, then cook for five minutes longer. Remove from heat and add one (6 oz.) pkg. chocolate chips and 1-1/2 cups miniature marshmallows. Mix and drop on wax paper.

VINEGAR PIE

2 tabsp. butter
1/2 cup sugar
3 tabsp. flour
1 teasp. cinnamon
1/4 teasp. cloves
1/4 teasp. allspice
1/8 teasp. salt
1 egg
2 tabsp. vinegar
1 cup water
1/2 recipe plain pastry

Cream butter and sugar. Add dry ingredients, egg, vinegar, and water. Cook in top of double boiler until thickened, stirring constantly. Line pie pan with pastry, bake in moderate 350 degree oven for three minutes, then pour in filling and continue baking until crust is brown.

Spanish Moss, gently flowing from huge old oak trees in or around the coastal areas, adds a sense of mystery and melancholy to South Mississippi. Moss grows especially well in cypress, oak and crepe myrtle trees.

Hattiesburg

In the 1990s, Hattiesburg was rated sixth in a national survey for overall livability for cities under 100,000. Shortly thereafter, the United States Conference of Mayors awarded Hattiesburg their prestigious "Livability Award." The old Southern saying, "Where there's smoke...." is applicable here, for with so much talk about this town, the talk is sure to ring true.

Hattiesburg, called the Hub City, is surely the hub of activity for South Mississippi, and one of the state's most progressive cities. Hattiesburg is proud to be the hometown of the sprawling University of Southern Mississippi --called simply "Southern" by alums. The university is known for many things, but rumor has it that commercial artists who hold a degree from USM are in demand by big advertising agencies.

On the campus, the All-American Rose Garden features 750 hybrid-T and Grandiflora bushes. USM's Danforth Chapel features seven handmade stained glass windows that portray the seven virtues. The USM Museum of Art exhibits noted Mississippi artists Walter Anderson and Marie Hull, among many, as well as a print collection that spans the history of art.

The de Grummond Children's Literature Collection at USM's McCain Library and Archives is most impressive and inspiring. Named for USM faculty member Lena de Grummond who founded the collection in 1966, there are now 55,000 volumes in the collection, with 1200 authors and illustrators represented. Emphasis is on American and British works, and that includes 200 versions of Cinderella and 150 versions of Little Red Riding Hood. Amazingly, there's an edition of Aesop's Fables, published in 1530.

Though you won't find any antebellum (pre-Civil War) structures in Hattiesburg, you will find many fine Victorian homes in the Historic District. Most of the houses there were built in the mid-1880s through the 1920s. The new and highly acclaimed Lake Terrace Convention Center has historic district driving tour information, and they'll tell you about "The Spirit That Builds," a 167-ft. circular mural that hangs in the rotunda of the Hattiesburg Library. The panels that comprise the mural depict the history of Hattiesburg, and perhaps we'll learn more about the woman "Hattie" for whom the town was named.

Speaking of Hattiesburg women, here's one who deserves special recognition for her generosity of spirit. In 1995, the 86-year old laundress, Miss Osceola McCarty, donated her life's savings to the University of Southern Mississippi for a scholarship fund. Those for whom she'd washed and ironed had no idea Miss Osceola, who had a sixth grade education, was saving her money for a worthy cause. This generous soul paid no attention to the media furor her gift caused, and gave little notice to the honorary doctorate from Harvard. Miss McCarty said in a previous interview: *"People tell me that I am a hero, but I don't feel that way. I'm just proud I'm leaving something positive in this world. My only regret is that I didn't have more to give."*

Osceola McCarty's gift of $150,000 continues to provide for others the education she always wanted but never got. The remarkable Miss McCarty is now deceased, but her dignity and generous nature will live on.

About 12 miles south of Hattiesburg on Highway 49, there's Camp Shelby and the Armed Forces Museum. This interesting museum houses more than 6,000 artifacts from each of the military branches who defended their nation in all its wars.

Since Hattiesburg is "coastal" in attitude and food, many of the recipes for this area will be combined with the Gulf Coast.

Brookhaven and McComb

Though these towns are separated by about 25 miles, they are often looped together as a destination. Both are known as quiet, pretty towns that have the amenities sought by retirees. **Brookhaven** boasts an historic Victorian district, and the historic Whitworth College campus, which is scheduled to open soon as the new Mississippi School of the Arts. Hailing from Brookhaven is Bob Pittman, founder of Music Television Video (MTV) in 1981. Pittman's brother Tom is a Mississippi newspaperman.

McComb has a musical connection, as well as the place you'll find the Jerry Clower Museum, open by appointment. The R and B musician Bo Diddley, very popular in the late 1950s and 60s, is from McComb, and so is the guitarist Vasti Johnson. More recently, the triple-platinum young female singer, Brandy, calls McComb home. Outdoor enthusiasts will appreciate the Bogue Chitto Water Park and the Percy Quin State Park, both near McComb.

CHEESE STRAWS

2 cups sifted flour
1 tabsp. butter
Dash of red pepper
1 teasp. salt

Mix ingredients together; add one cup of grated cheese, and enough ice water to make a stiff dough (about six tablespoons). Roll and fold five times, buttering surface each time (using extra butter). Roll this and cut with pastry cutter or knife. Place in pan not letting the straws touch. Bake in a moderate oven. Remove from pan and let cool, then serve.

-From Miss Georgia Hopkins' Recipe Collection

SPICY CATFISH AMANDINE

1/4 cup butter, melted
3 tabsp. lemon juice
6 (6 oz.) catfish fillets
1-1/2 teasp. Creole seasoning
1/2 cup sliced almonds

Combine butter and lemon juice; dip each fillet in butter mixture; arrange in 13 x 9 x 2-inch baking dish. Sprinkle fish with Creole seasoning and almonds. Bake at 375 degrees for 25-30 minutes or until fish flakes easily when tested with fork. Serves 4-6.

BEST BRUSSELS SPROUTS

1/2 cup water
1 chicken-flavored bouillon cube
1 (10 oz.) pkg. frozen brussels sprouts
1/2 cup finely chopped onion
2 tabsp. tarragon vinegar

Place water in medium saucepan. Bring to boil and add bouillon cube; stir until dissolved. Add brussels sprouts; return to boil. Cover, reduce heat, and simmer for about five minutes, or until tender. Drain. Add onion and vinegar, stirring gently. Cover and chill several hours. Stir gently before serving. Serves 4.

JUDGE PETER'S PUDDING

Arrange in layers in dish:
3 sliced bananas
2 oranges
6 walnuts, broken into pieces
5 figs, cut in pieces
5 dates, cut in pieces

Mix and pour over layers:
1 box plain gelatine dissolved in
1/2 pint cold water
5/8 pint boiling water
2 cups sugar
Juice of 3 lemons

When pudding is cold, serve with whipped cream.

-From *"The Modern Priscilla"* Magazine, May, 1915

The Mississippi Gulf Coast

"The Coast" as it's known to native Mississippians, has long been the place to go for a little relaxation and night life. Cool breezes, local color, an abundance of delicacies from the sea --and an atmosphere that's now as much Las Vegas as Mississippi Gulf Coast-- is what you can count on once you arrive. Twelve big casino resort complexes are now at home on the Coast. The Beau Rivage Resort is listed among the top 100 hotels in the USA and Canada. You won't miss the neon lights and traffic, so directions to the casinos are not necessary. Just head south toward the water, and you'll soon arrive. You will also see the 65-ft. landmark Biloxi Lighthouse, which has guided ships to safe harbor since 1848. About 26 golf courses are available along the coast, as well, including Grand Bear, a Jack Nicklaus signature course listed by Golf Digest as one of the Top Ten Best New Golf Courses in the U.S.

The Gulf Coast stretches 55 miles along the heel of the state, from Pascagoula to the east to Waveland to the west, and in between, 26 miles of white sand beaches offer sunning, swimming, parasailing, windsurfing, and many other opportunities to get wet in salt water. At least three major attractions will give you an education on Mississippi's seacoast. These attractions are in the biggest towns, **Biloxi** and **Gulfport**, though it's hard to tell when you leave one town and enter another.

The J.L Scott Marine Education Center and Aquarium in Biloxi is a good place to start, with its 44,000-gallon tank aquarium and live displays of coastal zone animals. The Maritime and Seafood Industry Museum, also in Biloxi, houses important coastal photographs, artifacts, and a film on the devastation of Hurricane Camille. The Marine Life Oceanarium in Gulfport features a dolphin and sea lion show, underwater dive shows, and more.

Biloxi's "Mad Potter" is about to be at the center of a major museum of art designed by noted architect Frank Gehry, who also designed the outstanding Guggenheim Museum in Bilbao, Spain. The "Mad Potter" is a name given himself by potter George E. Ohr (1857-1918). Though he was primarily ignored in his lifetime, Ohr is now considered the father of American art pottery and his work is highly prized, if it can be found outside the Smithsonian or the Metropolitan Museum of Art. Ohr made paper-thin pottery which he treated like pie dough, manipulating the surface into angular folds. He used a fine, ground clay that is no longer available, and he believed that his un-glazed works were his best.

Expected to be completed in 2004, the Ohr-O'Keefe Museum of Art will be the only museum in the U.S. dedicated to a single potter. O'Keefe is former Biloxi Mayor Jeremiah O'Keefe, who raised about $7 million of the $16 million project. The art museum will no doubt continue to keep the Coast in the art spotlight.

Beautiful **Bay St. Louis,** the oldest coast community, was once the vacation site for planters from Natchez and aristocrats from New Orleans. It's easy to see why they congregated here: sea air, cool breezes, and stunning scenery for starters.

On the other end of the beach sits **Ocean Springs,** an arts community that boasts the Walter Anderson Museum. Anderson was a Mississippi painter whose work now enjoys an international prominence. His brother James started Shearwater Pottery in 1928, and family members continue the tradition of creating wonderful pottery at the family compound.

In between these towns find the pretty **Pass Christian** (Coasters say Cris-t-ann), where many rich New Orleanians built summer homes in the 1800s. The second oldest yacht club in the country provides endless photo opportunities. Wherever you go on the Coast, expect it to be crowded, because the Mississippi Gulf Coast has been named the number three in "Up and Coming" destinations, according to ASTA travel agents.

Less crowded is a series of barrier islands six miles off the coast of Ocean Springs, which make up the Gulf Islands National Seashore, determined by the U.S. Congress to be a national park area. The landscape on the islands is virtually unspoiled, and it's quite possible to see azure water and bright white sand beaches here. The islands are East Ship, West Ship (Ship Island was cut in half by Hurricane Camille in 1969), Horn and Petit Bois. Though primitive camping is available on all the islands, West Ship is the most developed. It offers picnic areas with showers, lifeguards, and swimming.

The Gulf Islands National Seashore Visitors Center is at Davis Bayou, 3500 Park Road. It has interpretive exhibits, nature trails, ranger programs, and more. To reach Ship Island if you don't have a boat, there are commercial ferries departing twice daily from Biloxi and Gulfport.

With all the activity on the coast, food is the fuel that keeps up the energy level, and there's no shortage of superb seafood. In fact, there's a September festival dedicated to coast cuisine; it's called the Annual Chefs of the Coast Food and Wine Festival, where more then 60 chefs create great gourmet food representing various influences including Cajun, Creole, Italian and French. See below a few recipes that may not qualify as gourmet, but when served up with all the trimmings, they comprise what many of us know and love as "Coast cuisine."

PARTY CHEESE SPREAD

1 lb. sharp cheese
12 green onions, chopped
1 cup slivered almonds, toasted
1 lb. bacon, cooked crisp
2 cups mayonnaise
Salt, red pepper to taste

Mix ingredients well; cover and chill. Serve with party crackers.

GULFPORT SALAD

2 cups crabmeat
4 stalks celery
8 tabsp. mayonnaise
4 hard-boiled eggs
16 shrimp, stuffed with olives and capers

Chop celery and mix with mayonnaise and crabmeat. Place mixture in four generous lettuce cups. Garnish with boiled eggs, quartered, and stuffed shrimp. Serves 4. Easy and good luncheon dish.

BILOXI SEAFOOD CASSEROLE

1 lb. shrimp, peeled, deveined
1 lb. scallops
3 tabsp. butter
1 lb. crabmeat
2 cups cooked rice
1-1/2 cups V8 juice
1-1/2 cups mayonnaise
1/3 cup bell pepper, chopped
Salt and pepper to taste

Saute shrimp and scallops in butter until heated through, but not fully cooked (about two minutes). Blend remaining ingredients, pour into 8 x 11 inch pan, then bake in pre-heated 350 degree oven for about 30 minutes. Serves 6 to 8.

LOBSTER PIE

2 lbs. lump lobster meat
4 oz. butter
3 oz. dry sherry
1 qt. rich cream sauce
Salt, pepper, nutmeg to taste
Pie crust to cover

Sauté lobster in butter for five minutes. Pour in wine and boil three minutes. Add cream sauce and bring mixture to boil. Add seasonings to taste. Pour into deep dish casserole and cover with pie crust. Bake at 375 degrees until crust is browned, about 20 minutes. Serves 4.

GULF OYSTER CHOWDER

1 pint oysters
1/2 cup finely chopped onion
1/4 cup finely chopped celery
1/4 cup finely chopped green pepper
2 tabsp. butter
1 cup light cream
1/2 cup tomato sauce
1 (4 oz.) can sliced mushrooms, drained
1/3 cup rice, cooked
2 tabsp. dry sherry
1 tabsp. snipped parsley
1/2 teasp. salt, pepper to taste
1/4 teasp. ground nutmeg

Drain oysters; reserve liquid; add water to make one cup. Chop oysters. In saucepan, simmer oysters in the liquid for about five minutes or until edges begin to curl. Remove from heat.

In another saucepan, cook onion, celery, and green pepper in butter until tender but not brown. Add vegetables to cooked oysters along with cream, tomato sauce, mushrooms, rice, sherry, parsley, salt, pepper, and nutmeg. Heat through. Season to taste and serve immediately. Serves 4.

BLACKENED CATFISH

Catfish fillets
1/2 cup unsalted butter, melted
Cajun spices
Lemon juice
Garnish with lemon slices
Chopped parsley

Preheat a cast-iron skillet until hot. Dredge catfish fillets in melted butter; place in skillet skin side down; cook for about 3-1/2 or 4 minutes. Turn fillet, season generously with Cajun spices and cook an additional 3 to 3/12 minutes, until edges blacken. Remove to heated serving plate; season with lemon juice, garnish with lemon slices and parsley. Serves 4.

DEVILED CRAB AT THE PASS

1/2 lb. fresh crab meat
1 clove garlic
1/2 green pepper, cut in strips
1 teasp. onion, diced
1 red pimento, chopped
1 cup sauterne
1 hard-boiled egg, chopped
Dash of cayenne pepper
1/2 teasp. dry mustard
1/2 cup flour
1/4 lb. butter
1 quart fish broth

Sauté onion, garlic, pepper together; cook until done but not browned. Blend in flour, then add fish broth and remaining ingredients. Mix thoroughly. Serve in crab shells either hot or cold. Serves 4.

CRAWFISH FETTUCINE

3 sticks butter
3 onions, chopped
2 green bell peppers, chopped
3 stalks celery, chopped
3 lbs. crawfish tails
3 cloves garlic, minced
1 tabsp. parsley, chopped
1/2 cup flour
1 pint cream (Half and Half)
1 lb. jalapeno cheese, cubed
12 oz. bag fettucine

Sauté onion, bell pepper, and celery until tender. Add crawfish tails and simmer ten minutes, stirring often. Add next four ingredients and mix well. Simmer for 30 minutes, stirring occasionally. Add jalapeno cheese and stir until melted. Meanwhile, cook noodles, drain, and cool. Combine noodles and sauce. Pour into a big, greased casserole dish (6 qt.). Bake uncovered in a 300 degree oven for 20 minutes or until heated through. Serves 12.

PASTA SALAD WITH SHRIMP

Bag (30 oz.) bow tie pasta
2 lbs. medium shrimp
1 bell pepper
1 red bell pepper
2 tabsp. parsley, chopped
1 bunch green onions, sliced (green tops, too)
2/3 cup vinaigrette dressing

Cook pasta according to package directions, slightly firm. Peel and devein shrimp, grill or broil until done. Roast, deseed, and chop bell peppers. Toss all ingredients with viniagrette. Serves 10.

BAKED TOMATOES BAY ST. LOUIS

4 large, ripe tomatoes
8 tabsp. butter or margarine
1/2 cup finely minced onion
2 cloves garlic, minced
1 teasp. Worcestershire sauce
Dash hot sauce (Tabasco)
2 teasp. mustard (Dijon)
Salt and pepper to taste
4 teasp. fresh minced parsley
3/4 cup white bread crumbs

Cut tomatoes in half crosswise. Place cut side up in shallow baking dish. Melt half the butter in skillet; saute onions and garlic until tender. Stir in next four ingredients. Sprinkle all over cut tomatoes. Melt remaining butter, add coarse bread crumbs and parsley. Sprinkle this mixture over tomatoes. Bake in pre-heated oven at 350 until heated through, about 15 minutes. Serves 4.

Beauvoir; read about it in the Mississippiana Chapter.

Chapter 7
Mississippiana

Since "Mississippiana" is not in the dictionary, to the best of my knowledge, perhaps we can define it here. To me, the word means the most interesting, the most unique, the most 'Mississippi' of all the things in our state. It's the best of all those special nuances that make us want to say, "This is who we are and what we do — and we're pleased with ourselves for pulling it off."

Mississippiana is the Natchez Trace, the Blues Highway, Pilgrimages, the way we love our country stores and old camphouses; it's the fact that we care enough to comfort the bereaved family by bringing food to help soothe the hurt and help feed the out-of-towners who came for the funeral; it's the weddings that seem to get bigger each year, even though the marriages may not last long enough to pay for the bride's big event; it is the Neshoba County Fair and our own serene and lovely State Parks; it's the St. Paddy's Parade in Jackson and the Old Capitol Museum, and the Belhaven district, where Miss Eudora lived. Mississippiana is Beauvoir, the coastal home that honors the memory of our own Jefferson Davis; it's watching the sun set across the Mississippi River from the bluff above Natchez Under the Hill; it's cruising the rivers on Sunday afternoons, sometimes with picnics and coolers. Mississippiana is Elvis in all his glory, for he's the home-town boy who made the biggest splash; it's the pretty girls and delicate elderly ladies who dress up in lovely gowns that would make Miss Scarlett swoon as they greet Pilgrimage guests each year; it's the marvelous old mansions dressed to the nines because "compny's comin'." It is family reunions and class reunions and picnics at the lake. It's coming home from school to the aroma of a freshly-baked cake.

Mississippiana is all the great old restaurants that may not look so hot from the outside, but they are traditions held dear by those who frequent them. When entertainers and dignitaries send their private planes to Doe's in Greenville to bring back hot tamales or some such specialty of the place, they don't mind that it looks like a dilapidated old store front, because that's the way it's always been. It has a reputation, and it is traditional. Everything mentioned above is Mississippiana, and that's what we love about the state.

This last chapter gives us a closer look at what we think makes up "Mississippiana" — the unique places and things we hold near and dear.

The Mississippi State Capitol

This impressive Beaux Arts-style building is where Mississippi is governed and it remains one of the most architecturally-significant structures in the South. The "new capitol" is the state's second capitol; the first one, begun in 1839, now houses the state's Historical Museum. The new capitol was built between 1901 and 1903 at a cost of $1,093,641; it was repaired and redecorated in 1934-35, and completely restored between 1979 and 1982 at a cost of $19 million. Original construction was funded by back taxes owed the state by the Illinois Central Railroad.

Architect Theodore Link of St. Louis spared no expense in creating Mississippi's house of government. The design of the building was patterned after the national capitol in Washington, DC. The capitol —including three floors and a rotunda— was built to comfortably accommodate three branches of government: the Legislative, Judicial, and Executive, though the judicial branch has since been moved to a nearby building. The interior walls are marble, with a base of Belguim black marble.

The rotunda is particularly stunning with white Italian marble walls rising up from a base of New York jet black marble. Eight massive columns are man-made art marble, while the balustrades are cast iron. The four scenes in the dome represent native American Indians (two scenes), a Spanish explorer, and a Confederate general. The rotunda practically sparkles with gold gilt, stained glass, and 750 lights. Atop the rotunda rests a solid copper eagle measuring 8 ft. high x 15 ft. wide. The eagle is coated with gold leaf.

Tours of the capitol are available on the hour between 9AM and 3:30PM Monday through Friday; there is no charge. For group tour appointments, call 601/359-3114.

The Governor's Mansion

The beautiful mansion the governor calls home was completed in 1842 at a cost of about $61,000. Architect William Nichols designed the Greek Revival-style mansion and it remains a showplace for the state. The classic lines represent dignity and simplicity, which was the intention of the architect. It was designed primarily to accommodate state functions and visiting dignitaries as well as personal quarters for the governor and his family. Today, it is the second oldest continuously occupied gubernatorial residence in the United States.

Interior furnishings are lovely and tasteful, but not opulent. Antique furnishings abound, and they are offset by crystal chandeliers, Corinthian columns, elegant draperies and rich wall colors in rose, golds, greens, cream, and pumpkin. The room most often associated with state functions is the Gold Parlor, a spacious sitting room that is appointed with Empire furnishings, including sofas by the inimitable cabinetmaker Duncan Phyfe. Adjoining is the State Dining Room. It features lush crown molding in a cream color, which lets the gold wall color remain dominant. A table and sixteen high-back chairs are ready for entertaining important guests.

An unbelievable incident occurred in 1904. The legislature considered disposing of the Governor's Mansion to allow for commercial development, though their plans were quickly changed when they saw the public's reaction. Voters were adamant, so the legislature allocated funding for a major restoration. In the 1940s, the yellow brick exterior was painted white, and in 1944, the State Building Commission authorized the purchase of historic furnishings. In 1971, structural deterioration warranted vacating the building for a $2.7 restoration which called for restoring the mansion to its original state. After much research and documented purchases, the U.S. Department of the Interior named the mansion a National Historic Landmark.

Tours are conducted on the half-hour Tuesday through Friday from 9:30 until 11:00 AM, except during official state functions. The mansion is located at 300 East Capitol.

The Natchez Trace

Though the Natchez Trace Parkway, called simply "The Trace" by Mississippians, cuts through a corner of Alabama and meanders a bit into Tennessee, we think of it as belonging exclusively to Mississippi. The 400-mile parkway is clean and green, bill-board free, and one of the most scenic routes in the United States.

This is one very old road. According to some sources, buffalo tramped the trail about 8,000 years ago, and later, native Americans used the path for their hunting and tracking expeditions. The route became more consistently used in the 1700s, when the French and the Spanish explorers and soldiers arrived. By the late 18th century, men from the midwest who floated their goods down the Mississippi River to sell in New Orleans and Natchez, began using the old "Indian Trail" to get back home. They sold their makeshift vessels and looked for the easiest route back home.

Soon, the Indian Trail was the most heavily travelled wilderness road in the new country. Wild animals, hostile Indians, roving bandits, and disease took their toll on the overland travelers, so the new steamboats on the Mississippi River were most welcome for men traveling north toward home.

Post riders, an early version of the Pony Express, used the trail as a mail route in the early 1800s, though by the late 1820s, the trail was a forgotten hardship. In 1909, the Mississippi Chapter of the Daughters of the American Revolution undertook the work of marking the old trail, which became a major project that resulted in the Natchez Trace Parkway.

Today, the pristine and pretty Natchez Trace Parkway is well worth the time it takes to drive it. The Trace is maintained, administered, and patrolled by the National Park Service of the U.S. Department of the Interior.

Markers along the way tell the fascinating story of the Trace and the early Americans who used it. Along the way, you're treated to the most unspoiled public place in our crowded country, where you can expect to see wild game —deer and turkey are apt to amble across the highway at any time— towering trees, flat fields and meadowlands, clear streams, and abundant wild flowers. The Trace provides an opportunity to slow down and enjoy nature's wonders, for the speed limit is a strictly enforced 50 MPH.

At the south end of the Trace, learn that in its heyday, the old frontier trail had "stands," or inns, that were built to accommodate the trail travelers. At mile marker 15.5, just north of Natchez, see Mount Locust Inn, built around 1780.

Mount Locust is the only survivor of about 50 such inns, which were located about one day's walk apart. For 25 cents, a traveler could enjoy a supper of "mush and milk" and have the privilege of sleeping under a roof, though often on the floor with countless others.

The Mississippi Crafts Center at **Ridgeland,** mile marker 102.4, exhibits and sells the work of Mississippi artists. It is housed in a quaint log cabin, with rocking chairs on the front porch. **Kosciusko,** north of Ridgeland, is a wonderful Trace town, with a welcome center and museum honoring the town's namesake the first stop. The town is built around a Courthouse square, with quaint and cute shops lining the street. This town is the birthplace of Oprah Winfrey; her first church is now a community center for the Buffalo United Methodist Church.

Head north up the Trace and find **French Camp,** home of the Christian boarding school founded in 1885, French Camp Academy. The Huffman Log Cabin serves as a visitor's center and gift shop, with local arts and crafts for sale. The Colonel James Drane House is open Monday-Saturday. Drane began construction of the house in 1846. Today, it has been restored and furnished with antiques. Also in French Camp is Rainwater Observatory, the largest public access observatory in the state; open year 'round.

Just north of **Tupelo,** the Natchez Trace Parkway Headquarters and Visitors Center at mile 266 is a museum of the Trace. It offers artifacts and displays and an audio-visual exhibit. At the north end of the Mississippi portion of the Trace, enter the foothills of the Appalachian Mountains, where a stop at Tishomingo State Park will show even more natural beauty and nature trails. There's an old rope pedestrian bridge high up over a swift river below, which is a great treat for children.

The Trace provides picnic areas and rest stops with clean facilities, and easy access to nearby towns, but the only service station on the Trace is at mile marker 193.9, located at Jeff Busby State Park. Enjoy this early link to civilization! It is indeed a Mississippi treasure.

Pilgrimages

It is my personal belief that the epic film, *Gone With the Wind,* did for Mississippi Pilgrimages what Walt Disney did for animation. The 1939 film that starred Vivian Leigh and Clark Gable depicted, in living color, what some folks call "Southern mystique," and that includes grand mansions, romance, a war that tore apart families and friendships, desperation, life-altering changes, and finally, survival. Not only did the stalwart people survive, but so did many of the marvelous old mansions, and now they're cherished and celebrated as the architectural art and historical documentation that they surely are.

Natchez first began to officially invite guests to the homes in 1931, when the Mississippi Federation of Garden Clubs held its annual meeting in the town. There are two stories about the event, and I am not certain which is entirely accurate. I like to think that perhaps a bit of both may be true. One story says that garden club members offered tours as a way to promote history and heritage; the other says that the state garden clubbers planned to view the gardens of Natchez when a late freeze killed all the blooms, so they invited the guests to tour the homes instead. Whatever, the homes were toured and the response was so favorable, a larger event was planned for 1932.

The ladies of Natchez embarked upon a nationwide publicity campaign, complete with one of their own, Katherine Grafton Miller, touting the charm of Old Natchez in various cities. It worked, for people came in droves the second year.

On that first organized tour in early April of 1932, twenty-four houses were opened and visitors came and fell in love with the lovely homes of history. And then, when *Gone With the Wind* was released, a new appreciation for the grand old homes emerged, and Natchez became a popular place.

Other Mississippi towns followed suit, and today, the best known Pilgrimage tour towns are Natchez, Columbus, Holly Springs and Vicksburg. At Pilgrimage time, which usually coincides with the blossoming of spring flowers, ladies in festive period costume greet guests who come to take a look at living history. Thanks to preservation efforts and a renewed interested in antiques and architecture, Mississippi Pilgrimages are getting better each year.

An artist's sketch of a grand mansion.

Historic Preservation

Down South, historic preservation has many monikers. Some towns use the term for downtown development; others use it when a single house is restored. The restoration project could be a water tower, an old bridge, or a dilapidated opera house. Usually in Mississippi, historic preservation generally refers to a house, preferably an antebellum, meaning "before the war," and in this case, the Civil War. The consensus is that we lose our sense of place when we lose our landmarks, therefore we make every effort to save them. Sense of place is important to Southerners; it's about who we are.

In the 1930s, a federal government office decided to document noteworthy buildings across the country through what they called the Historic American Buildings Survey (HABS). The results of the survey gave preservationists an inkling of what needed preserving, and it gave some the impetus to start preserving. It was soon learned that the South was rife with important structures other than Mount Vernon and Monticello.

Many old houses in Mississippi were by then peeling and reeling, since after the Civil War and Reconstruction, there was little money left to spruce them up. Then came World War I, the Great Depression, and World War II, so preservation was put on hold for a long time. Unfortunately, by the time preservation was again taken seriously in the 1960s, so many of the treasures were by then lost, either from falling down or being torn down to make room for a parking lot or convenience store. Natchez, however, did a better job of salvaging what they had, and they in turn started the first Pilgrimage in the state.

People came to see the homes of history during those early years of Pilgrimage, and they apparently loved what they saw. They saw architectural grace and grandeur, much of which had been created by skilled craftsmen who used only pattern books, for architects were scarce in the early to mid-1800s in some of Mississippi's remote regions.

And still they come today. They look up at the tall columns and wonder how they were so carefully crafted and then placed so securely without cranes and power tools. The columns represent the Greek Revival style, which was the most widespread and popular architectural style of the mid-1800s. The opulent style was not entirely for show, though many of the planters and others who built them wanted to show their wealth. There was often a utilitarian reason for the recessed porches and thick columns and pediments, and that reason was comfort. Such design features provided shade from the hot Southern sun, and blockage from the cold winter winds.

Thanks to preservationists and those who promote heritage tourism as a viable vacation option, the South is now holding on to what's left. Historic foundations are springing up in many towns and cities, and they're serious about the work they've undertaken, which, we hope, is restoring the properties to their original state. There's something sad about a lovely old home that is nothing but a shell of what it once was. Modern conveniences are fine and we're all spoiled for them, but we hope they aren't at the expense of the integrity of a marvelous old structure, lovingly built so long ago. Since historic preservation is now attracting huge investments, surely the homes of history will survive to teach us just a little more about the way things were.

Neshoba County Fair

There's nothing else, anyplace, like the Neshoba County Fair. This Mississippi tradition becan in 1889 when fair-goers arrived in covered wagons to visit family and old friends. Over the years, politicians discovered its value, and now, the Neshoba County Fair —called by *National Geographic* Mississippi's Giant Houseparty—is a must-stop to stump for every statewide politician who expects to be elected.

According to the National Register of Historic Places nomination form, in the early days of the Fair, it was a one-day event in a pine grove. Shortly thereafter, oak trees were planted in a square formed by rows of houses. After the turn of the century, the midway, the racetrack, and "subdivisions" were developed to allow for more cabins. Before the 1920s, there were two framed hotels on Founders' Square, but the hotel system soon gave way to the hospitality of the cabin owners.

The Neshoba County Fairgrounds near Philadelphia is the place to be for a week each summer in late July-early August. It's even better if you're lucky enough to have a cabin, though that's not likely unless the cabin has been in your family for eons. There are about 600 of these play-house cabins, and they are indeed prize possessions.

For most of the year, those gaily-painted, festive cabins —some say camp-houses— look like a deserted town on a movie back-lot in Hollywood. But during fair days, the camphouse town comes alive with motion, music, and the finest in good old Mississippi food. Old friends and new ones sit on the front porches of the cabins, watching the crowds go by, with flags and banners flapping in the breeze from the electric fans on the porches.

The Neshoba County Fair is a typical country fair with merry-go-rounds and painted ponies, ferris wheels, and midway exhibits —but it's quite special in that thousands of "day visitors" appear to spend the day, while the camptown atmosphere of the cabins last well into the night.

And then there are political speeches, band concerts, prayer meetings, flea markets, talent contests, big-name entertainment, and horse racing. Every afternoon, the race track is filled with fans of harness racing, madly applauding and cat-calling as the racers streak around the course. This is the only licensed racetrack in Mississippi.

In the center of camp town is Founders' Square, where the roof is nature's own green leaves, and the floor is sawdust over earth. Sofas are benches built around the trees, usually filled with people visiting, sometimes recalling previous fairs and passed-on people. For a real Mississippi experience, don't miss the Neshoba County Fair!

MISSISSIPPI
HOUSE PARTY

Beauvoir
Last Home of Jefferson Davis

Though Jefferson Davis was born near Fairview, Kentucky in 1808, Mississippi proudly claims him. When he was two years old, his family moved to Woodville, MS, and built the home Rosemont. Jefferson was the youngest of ten children. The Davis family called Rosemont home until 1895. It still stands today, one mile east of Woodville, on MS. Highway 24. The home is privately owned.

Jefferson Davis was an American patriot whose impressive credentials include graduating from the U.S. Military Academy at West Point, serving as an officer in the U.S. Army, a U.S. Congressman, a U.S. Senator, U.S. Secretary of War, and later, the only president of the Confederacy.

While at West Point, Davis's friends included Leonidas Polk and Robert E. Lee. Perhaps it was the military academy that gave Davis the idea of States' rights. After graduation, 2nd Lt. Davis met and fell in love with the daughter of his base commander, Sarah Knox Taylor, who died of malaria shortly after their marriage and subsequent move to Mississippi. The heartbroken Davis remained in seclusion for years, until he met Miss Varina Howell of Natchez.

As a newcomer to politics, the eloquent Davis made friends in high places. After hearing Davis speak, John Quincy Adams said that Davis was not an ordinary man, and that he would go far in American politics.

Davis was serving in the U.S. Senate when Mississippi seceded from the Union in January, 1861. In less than two weeks, he resigned from the Senate. On February 10, 1861, he received word that he had been elected President of the Confederate States of America. He was inaugurated February 18 in Montgomery, Alabama, though the Confederate government was moved to Richmond, Virginia, three months later. The next few years were turbulent, indeed.

When General Robert E. Lee surrendered at Appomattox on April 9, 1865, Davis and other members of his cabinet headed South, though Davis was captured by the Union Army in Irwinville, Georgia. The date was May 10, 1865. Jefferson Davis was imprisoned on May 22. He was accused of planning the assassination of President Lincoln, which was unfounded and untrue. Nevertheless, Davis was shackled in irons, treated harshly, and denied his U.S. citizenship for crimes he did not commit.

After prominent men from New York City and Washington, DC came to his defense, Davis was released from prison in May, 1867, but only after his friends put up a $100,000 bond. Among them were *New York Tribune* editor

Horace Greeley, Cornelius Vanderbilt, and Augustus Schell. After his release, the Davis family visited Canada, Wales, Scotland, and Continental Europe.

In 1877, Jefferson Davis, his wife Varina, and their youngest child Winnie visited the Mississippi Gulf Coast, where Davis finally found a place he could call home. It was at the lovely, beach-front home of family friend Mrs. Sarah Dorsey. Davis arranged to purchase Beauvoir (French for "beautiful view") and lived quietly with his family. It was here that he wrote *The Rise and Fall of the Confederate Government.* The former political leader of the Southern states remained at Beauvoir until his death in 1889, when he died while visiting friends in New Orleans. He still was not a U.S. citizen.

After Davis' death, Varina wrote *Jefferson Davis, A Memoir by His Wife.* She and Winnie struggled to keep Beauvoir until Varina's death. Even under financial duress, Mrs. Davis refused to sell Beauvoir to a promoter who planned to convert it to a hotel. Instead, she sold it for considerably less to the Mississippi Division, United Sons of Confederate Veterans, knowing that in their hands Beauvoir would continue to be a memorial to her late husband.

Initially, it was a memorial home for Confederate veterans, though in 1941, the grounds and main house were opened to the general public as a way to produce income for the upkeep. Today, the ground floor of the mansion is a Davis Family Museum, while a Confederate Museum occupies the old hospital building. More than 700 CSA veterans are interred at Beauvoir Cemetery, just a small percentage of the young men who died for their beliefs in the War for Southern Independence, as they call it at Beauvoir.

In 1978, President Jimmy Carter signed a bill to restore citizenship to Jefferson Davis. The bill passed the U.S. Congress without even one dissenting vote.

Beauvoir is a National Historic Landmark still owned and operated by the Sons of Confederate Veterans. It is located at 2244 Beach Blvd., Biloxi, and it is open for tours from 9AM until 5PM each day. Admission charged. A gift shop is on the premises.

The Origin of Memorial Day

An event occurred in Columbus in 1866 that helped to heal the wounds left smarting from the recent Civil War. A group of Columbus women met in the home Twelve Gables to plan a way to honor the war dead interred at the Odd Fellows Cemetery. Several hundred Confederate soldiers lay in rest, while about 40 Union graves were there, too. They had been wounded on nearby battlefields and transported to hospital in Columbus. It was hard to tell blue uniforms from gray in the smoke and confusion of war, and after all, they were all Americans and they needed help.

The women planned a day in April to cut flowers from their gardens and transport them to the cemetery for what they were calling Confederate Decoration Day. Once there, one of the women saw the neglected and over-grown Union graves, and said to her friends that the "Yankee" soldiers perhaps had wives, mothers, and sisters, too, so she placed a few flowers on the Union graves nearest her. Other ladies followed suit, and soon both Confederate and Union graves were adorned with lovely spring flowers.

News of this generous gesture spread by word of mouth and finally, a brief mention of it appeared in the *New York Tribune.* Young lawyer F.M. Finch saw the piece and was inspired to write the poem, *"The Blue and the Gray."* The poem first appeared in the September, 1867, issue of the *Atlantic Monthly* magazine, and after a while, Confederate Decoration Day evolved into the nation's Memorial Day, which we celebrate annually today. It is now a major springtime holiday.

Other towns across the South claim a Confederate Decoration Day, though according to the Library of Congress, Columbus, Mississippi, was the only town to honor Union soldiers, too. The federal soldiers were moved to Shiloh National Cemetery in 1867, though row after row of "Unknown Confederate Soldiers" still rest in peace in what is now Friendship Cemetery in Columbus, where Decoration Day is still observed each April.

First Monday Trade Day

Twelve times each year, the small town of Ripley in north Mississippi – between Holly Springs and Corinth— attracts thousands of people who come to partake of the goods at First Monday Trade Day. And those goods include most things you could possibly want —from dogs to daylilies —with merchandise provided by about 400 vendors who spread their wares over 50 acres. Expect to find some antiques, some junque, shoes, jeans, wicker furniture, animals, and a lot of surprises.

This event began in 1893, when local people gathered at the Courthouse Square to sell, trade, or barter their items. It was so successful, they decided to make it a monthly event, and it grew beyond their expectations.

Today, this giant flea market begins on the Saturday before the first Monday. Sunday is the biggest day, with vendors closing up shop on Monday. If you go, you're sure to find something you didn't know you needed.

There's also cafeteria-style food, a drink shop, a place to buy pizza, and a place to get a big slice of pie. To get specific directions from your location, call 1/800-RIPLEY.

Tailgate Parties

Though all the major universities have fabulous tail-gate parties after each daytime football game, Ole Miss appears to be the one that best represents Mississippi style and `elan. Tailgate parties at the Grove can be major productions. It's not unusual to see the fine family sterling --from ornate candelabra to opulent serving bowls-- in service at a tailgate party. Some tailgaters bring beautiful floral centerpieces, too, with all the food and folk protected from the elements by splendidly engraved canvas canopies. The more affluent who frequent the tailgate parties at the Grove sometimes bring their household staff to help serve and clear away. Others, however, prefer traditional picnic fare and less formal presentations, and they have a grand time, too.

At the Grove, you know where to find your friends, because the same people have the same place for each game. It's a territorial thing, according to active Grove-ites. The food varies from group to group, though it is difficult to serve food that must be hot from the oven. Burgers, sandwiches, salads, and picnic foods are easiest to manage, and usually topped off with an outstanding dessert.

TAILGATE'N IN STYLE!
RUSHING

Delta Blues

Not only does the Mississippi Delta produce bumper crops of cotton, it has produced more prominent blues musicians than any place else on earth. In fact, the blues were born and grew to maturity in the Delta. The amazing thing is that these pure American musicians became popular in Europe long before fans on this side of the Atlantic knew much about blues music. We knew B.B. King, but not many of us knew that "the father of Blues Music" was Robert Johnson. I had not heard the late great Son Thomas sing about..."My baby done got drown-ed," until I moved to north Mississippi. Most of us knew about Muddy Waters, but did we know that his real name is McKinley Morganfield?

My favorite is John Lee Hooker, born in Clarksdale in 1917. His first big hit was "Boogie Chillen," which hit the charts long before he was inducted into the Rock and Roll Hall of Fame. Hooker's music is hypnotic; it's full of raw blues and passion, with no pretense and no artificial polish. In 1989 --at the age of 72-- the legendary Hooker paired up with Santana and won his first Grammy for "The Healer." British rocker Eric Clapton, an expert on Hooker's music, emulated Hooker's style as he was developing his own. Others who studied Hooker's music include the Rolling Stones and ZZ Top.

Today, some of the legendary blues clubs have closed, but others have taken their places. Try One Block East in Greenville, the Airport Grocery in Cleveland, Po' Monkey's in Merigold, and the new Ground Zero in Clarksdale, which is owned by the actor Morgan Freeman, who also owns the restaurant Madidi's. Ask locals; they know where the blues can be heard on any given week-end, and if you want to wait for the big Delta Blues festivals and events, there's the Delta Blues Festival in Greenville in September; the new Highway 61 Blues Festival near Greenville in June; and the Sunflower River Blues and Gospel Festival in Clarksdale in August.

Until fairly recently, the Flowing Fountain in Greenville was a sure bet to hear the blues, though it is closed at this writing. Many years ago, a young married couple by the name of Ike and Tina Turner drew a SRO crowd when they appeared there.

The local Blues authority is the Delta Blues Museum in Clarksdale, which began in 1979 for the purpose of preserving and making accessible to the public information, programs, and related services concerning the history and significance of blues music. The old brick walls and wood of the former railroad depot that now houses the museum are perfect for displaying the collection of black and white art, which helps to explain the birth of the blues; see it capsulated in the following space.

"After the Civil War when the Mississippi Delta was a new frontier, freed African Americans came seeking the opportunities afforded by the rich soil and the timber industry. Black laborers filled the 'levee camps' and were pretty much isolated from the rest of the world. As a result of this isolation, they developed their own music --freely and for the first time-- without outside intervention. They remembered the musical traditions from their native Africa and incorporated a form of that sound into their own style. Thus, because of the conditions, the lifestyle, and the land, the blues were born."

Delta bluesmen perform at a Blues festival.

John C. Stennis Space Center

When NASA arrived on the Mississippi Gulf Coast in the 1960s, their mission was to test-fire the large rocket boosters that would, they hoped, propel Apollo astronauts to the moon. Such a feat required extensive property, a multitude of buildings, and a plethora of scientists. When the Apollo test program ended in the 1970s, the vacated space was available to be filled by others, and indeed it was. But with the advent of the space shuttle, NASA reactivated the engine testing facilities to test the space shuttle's main engines. The once-new tenants remained, however, and the Navy now has four major divisions located here: The Commander, Naval Meteorology, Oceanographic Command, and a Naval Research Lab.

But it is the NASA operation that gets more attention. The StenniSphere Museum and Visitors Center provides more than ample information, and treats you to the viewing of a space suit, moon rocks, and other interactive exhibits sure to create the interest of all ages. Visitors can tour the simulator and other aspects of the space program, but the reality check comes in when you hear the deafening roar of the testing of the 7,000 pound space shuttle engine. If the testing is a must for you, call first to see if your trip coincides with the testing schedule. The site, near Bay St. Louis off I-10, exit 2, has been named the "Travel Attraction of the Year." For information, dial 1/800-237-1821, or www.ssc.nasa.gov.

Legendary Mississippi Restaurants

This section presents a difficult task. There are so many fine restaurants in the Magnolia State, it would be impossible to mention them all in limited space. So we've decided to include those that have been around for a long time, and those that are particularly well-known statewide, based on informal polls of people who dine out often. Featured below are the restaurants our poll participants consider legendary.

Starting with the River Cities south, Natchez is first. If you like "Spring Chicken Southern Fried" served with tiny, tasty, crisp biscuits, have lunch at the **Carriage House,** which is on the grounds of the grand mansion Stanton Hall. Lunch is served daily, though it is open for dinner during Pilgrimage only. The garden club women who run this restaurant serve up the kind of food once served on the old plantations.

Vicksburg's **Walnut Hills** loads up a lazy-Susan with a big selection of vegetables, meats, and serves the Southern delicacies round-table style. **Goldie's Trail Barbecue** on South Washington Steet is famous for spicy, tasty barbeacue. It's a place you'll go back to at every opportunity.

Greenville is next, with one of Mississippi's most legendary restaurants, **Doe's,** as its anchor establishment. Rumor has it that this unpretentious place in an old store building serves the best steaks in the South, and it was a favorite of 'Southern boys" who made good, among them President Bill Clinton and Elvis Presley. We've heard they both loved Doe's hot tamales, with Elvis going so far as to send his private plane to get a bundle of tamales. Doe's serves dinner only.

If your next stop is Greenwood, you're in luck, for this is the home of the **Crystal Grill,** known for serving simply delicious Southern food since 1913. The Crystal Grill is an institution in the Delta, and one of my favorites in the world. Home-made pies have meringue so high and thick, you won't believe it's real. The Crystal serves three meals daily; closed Monday.

Lusco's, another Delta favorite in Greenwood, has occupied the same old store building since 1933, through there is talk about a possible move to another location. Great steaks and broiled pompano are specialties of the house. Serves dinner only Tuesday through Saturday.

Still in the Delta, the upmarket **KC's** in Cleveland is as close to gourmet as anything you'll find in these parts, with more than a hint of international cuisine. KC's also boasts a nice wine cellar with more than 500 labels from across the world. It is not cheap by Mississippi standards, but whatever you pay you'll probably consider it a bargain. End your meal with the best creme brulee in six states. Owners, the Joe family of Cleveland, are well-known restaurateurs in the region.

Just north of Cleveland, the tiny town of Merigold has a surprise in store. The surprise is to find **Crawdad's,** a superb place for dinner if you like Louisiana-style seafood served in a big, spacious, former railroad depot. The mayor of Merigold owns Crawdad's.

On I-55 north, the **Como Steak House** in the little town of Como has a reputation for serving up the best steaks in the South. Tourists come for the food, and to visit the restaurant located in an old turn-of-the-century building on Main Street.

Head southeast to Oxford and the fine restaurant called **City Grocery** downtown. It is a treat to find such sophisticated Continental cuisine in a small town restaurant, but it's here, and its reputation is excellent.

Continue on to Tupelo, and try the inimitable **Johnny's Drive In,** where the barbecue is second to none. Johnny's is the oldest restaurant in Tupelo, and eating there is a tradition. Curb service is still available, but you should go inside. Great homemade pie will make you plan many return trips to Johnny's, but not on Sundays, for Johnny's is closed. The sign at the door says, "Closed Sunday. Gone to Church." Johnny's is on E. Main, not too far from the Elvis attractions.

Columbus is home to **Pete's Restaurant,** serving breakfast and lunch since the 1930s. It is the only restaurant in these parts to have been featured in *The New York Times* travel section, though the loyal customers keep coming back not for the prestigious publicity, but for the good food and very reasonable prices. Closed Sunday. Open seven days each week and always crowded is **Ruben's Catfish House.** It is located just west of town, within seeing distance, and it sits directly on the old Tombigbee River. A recent expansion has added an upstairs bar and balcony, which allows for great river views. The food consists of a salad bar and your choice of potatoes, with excellent hushpuppies. Fresh Mississippi catfish is about the best you'll find, and that's what Ruben's serves.

Between Columbus and Meridian on Highway 45 find the **Ole Country Bakery** at Brooksville, known to be a wonderful bakery that also serves soup and sandwiches for lunch. It is run by the Mennonite ladies, who use only the freshest ingredients to produce their tasty morsels. The cake-like poppy seed bread is the best you'll find anywhere, and they offer a nice variety of home-made pies and cakes. Closed Sunday.

Weidmann's in Meridian must be the oldest in the state, since it has been serving food to Mississippians since 1870. From its austere beginnings as Felix Weidmann's fruit and vegetable stand, the restaurant evolved into what it is today. It's a place where old world European charm meets America, and a special perk is the photographs of movie stars and other celebrities who've dined there. The restaurant continues a tradition begun during World War II when butter was scarce: they place a little crock of their homemade peanut butter on every table. The house specialties are seafood and steak, with their famous Blackbottom Pie a real treat. Weidmann's serves breakfast, lunch and dinner daily. *EDITOR'S NOTE: Just before press time, we learned that Weidmann's had been sold. It is now undergoing extensive remodeling.*

Jackson has many favorite old restaurants, with some in the heart of downtown on Capitol Street. **The Elite** has been feeding Jackson's finest for more than 50 years. House favorites for lunch and dinner include veal cutlets and enchiladas. The Elite is closed on Sunday.

On West Capitol, **The Mayflower** has been a favorite of downtown Jackson workers since 1935. This popular restaurant and its good food has been featured in national magazines. Fresh fish is a specialty of the house, including red fish, red snapper, and pompano. The Mayflower is closed on Sunday.

Dennery's, open since 1948, remains in the same family. Though Greek fare is the specialty, prime rib and seafood are equally as good. Dennery's at I-55 and High Street, is closed on Sunday.

Primos offers fresh seafood and prime rib, cooked to perfection. A favorite on the menu is Italian Grilled Chicken. The name 'Primos' has a long-standing reputation with native Jacksonians; see the new location on Lakeland Drive.

Nick's on Lakeland Drive is not as old as some in Jackson, but over the years, it has honored the traditions set by fine restaurants everywhere. Steaks, seafood, and pasta is even better with a selection from Nick's impressive wine list. Nick's, too, is closed on Sunday.

Though rumors abound that this Mississippi instutution is about to close, as of this writing, it is still open and serving the same great food we've always counted on. About 30 minutes from Jackson is Mendenhall's **Revolving Tables** Restaurant. This superb setting in an old hotel has served lunch —boarding-house-reach style— since 1915. This restaurant is thought to have been the setting for Eudora Welty's novel, *The Ponder Heart.* Miss Welty attended Mississippi University for Women with the owner's mother. Present owners are third genera-

tion to run the place. Expect delicious down-home Southern food laden on lazy Susans! It's in downtown Mendenhall.
EDITOR'S NOTE: Unfortunately, after 87 years, the Revolving Tables has now closed its doors. Perhaps someone will continue the fine tradition.

Step back in time near Collins —actually the Mt. Olive community between Collins and Hot Coffee— into a world few of us can even imagine. It's a tranquil community of Old Order German Baptists, similar in lifestyle to the Amish. You won't see fast cars or flashy lights, for these people use horse and buggy or bicycles, and they make their own clothes and grow their own food. At **Martha's Kitchen,** food is prepared on an old wood burning stove, and it is served by candlelight and lamplight if you're still there after dark. Everything served in the rustic restaurant is grown or prepared on the Diehl family farm, even to the freshly churned butter. Guests are served by reservation only, and they have no phone. Bill and Edith Diehl are the contacts, write them at: 1462 Highway 532, Mount Olive, MS 39119.

If you're in or around McComb at lunchtime, follow the crowd to **The Dinner Bell** on Fifth Street, just off Highway 51 North. Join the boarding-house reach diners and reach out for great vegetables that taste like garden-grown, and other Mississippi favorite foods such as fried chicken, pork roast and more. Also from McComb, take Highway 98 east to Foxworth and find **Leatha's Bar-B-Q,** said by many in this part of the state to serve up the best barbecue in the entire world! Hours are limited, though, with Leatha serving lunch only each Thursday, Friday and Saturday.

The Gulf Coast boasts **Mary Mahoney's Old French House Restaurant,** and it tops the list of the greats on the Coast. Mary Mahoney's is the legendary courtyard restaurant, in a rambling old building originally constructed in 1737. Magnificent live oak trees, said to be 2,000 years old, add mystique to the Courtyard. Mary Mahoney's is as famous for its fine food as for its setting. Seafood, of course, is the house specialty. Superb is the word for this historically significant place, so reservations are recommended. Mary Mahoney's is in Biloxi, and it is one of many outstanding Coast restaurants. Closed on Sunday.

Fine cheese-making and grape research is on-going at Mississippi State University.

Old-Fashioned Favorite Foods

We're so health-conscious now, we seldom partake of delicious Southern fried chicken and gravy — or fried catfish and hushpuppies— and other things that we know we shouldn't eat, but do anyway at every opportunity. Most of our parents and grandparents ate such foods everyday, and they seasoned fresh garden vegetables with fat from bacon or fat-back. They cooked with lard; they used real sugar; they drank whole milk, and they didn't seem to have too many weight problems. The only overweight people I remember were those who had "glandular" disorders.

My grandmother, Big Mama to us, lived to be 95, and she was healthy for 94 years. Hard work was a way of life for her, for she was widowed at 40 with six children to raise. That was before electric appliances made our lives so easy, and before children had such a selection of clothing to be laundered. So by the time she did laundry, gardening, cooking, cleaning, and caring for the children, she got in enough calorie-burning physical activity to eat whatever she wanted. She was robust and strong, but not fat. However, she did not eat food that had preservatives or other chemicals, as we do today. We ingest preservatives along with the fast foods that wreak havoc on our metabolism, and then we sit immobile in front of computers or television screens.

Is it any wonder that most of us have acquired a few extra pounds? So let's rationalize and say that if we're going to be "softer" anyway, we'd may as well enjoy it by eating foods that give us comfort. Right? Perhaps if we eat healthily all week, then have one or two comfort meals on weekends, we won't be obese. Anyhow, who could write a book about Mississippi food without including a few of our old favorites?

My list includes:

Chicken 'n' Dumplings so rich and tender, almost like a stew.
Thanksgiving Cornbread Dressing, with cranberry sauce and fat hen.
Young spring Chicken, fried to a golden brown, with rice and gravy.
Flossie's Famous Chicken Pot Pie.
Turnip Greens from the garden, after the first fall dew has blessed their leaves.
Big Mama's Rutabegas, slow cooked and tender.
Aunt June's Fresh Snap Beans.
Stella's Steamed Cabbage, finely chopped and well-seasoned.
Mother's Okra and Tomato Gumbo, with lots of onion and red pepper.
A big green salad, with fresh tomatoes and other garden vegetables.
Dried Baby Lima Beans, slow-cooked and thick, with a ham hock.
Homemade Ice Cream.
Daddy's Pound Cake

A Closer Look at a Southern Culinary Delight: Chicken

There's history associated with the favorite Mississippi delicacy of fried chicken. Back when times were cleaner and leaner, chickens were staples used to feed families, thus they were raised for daily use. Many homes and yards boasted "chicken coops," "hen yards," "pullet pens," hen houses," and more.

In payment for their their daily diet of corn and table scraps, the chickens offered up eggs — that versatile oval-shaped phenomenon that provided breakfast, egg salad or fried egg sandwiches for lunch, and deviled egg trays for parties and funerals. And then, the chicken's ultimate contribution was to die a swift death, be plucked, cut up, and fried in an inch or so of lard in a black iron skillet, then served to the family for Sunday dinner— dinner being the main meal served right after church. Lucky was the one who got the "pully bone."

Other days, the chicken may find his way to the table in a big pot of chicken 'n' dumplings, chicken and rice, barbecued chicken, chicken pie, chicken soup, Brunswick stew, and other culinary delights created by the woman of the house. But nothing was more appreciated than fried chicken, complete with potatoes and gravy and fresh vegetables from the garden, and perhaps a lemon icebox pie for dessert.

SOUTHERN FRIED CHICKEN

About 3/4 cup flour
Salt to taste
Pepper to taste
1-1/2 teasp. paprika
2 lb. fryer, cut-up

Heat shortening or oil, which should be at least one-half inch deep. Place flour, salt, pepper and paprika in a brown paper bag. Add a few pieces of chicken, then twist top of bag and shake to coat evenly. Do not crowd; if chicken is crowded, add more oil. Fry in hot oil until light brown on both sides. Reduce heat and cook 25 minutes longer. To "crisp" chicken, turn heat higher the last five minutes. Serve with gravy and creamed potatoes or rice.

CHICKEN GRAVY

From pan where chicken was fried— preferably a black iron Dutch oven or black iron skillet— pour off all but about one tablespoon of oil. To the oil, add one tablespoon of flour, salt and pepper to taste; brown flour. Mix equal amounts of milk and water, about one cup. Pour slowly into flour mixture. Stir and cook until gravy is thick.

FRIED CATFISH

4 to 6 catfish fillets
Buttermilk
Salt and pepper to taste
White cornmeal
Vegetable oil to fry

Wash catfish; pat dry. Place fillets in a shallow pan and pour about two tablespoons of buttermilk over each; coat both sides, add salt and pepper to taste. Pour about two cups of corn meal into a bag or bowl, then coat fish thoroughly. Fry fish in hot oil until lightly browned. Don't crowd fish. Drain on brown paper bag. Serve with plenty of hushpuppies, French fries, coleslaw, and big slices of onion.

MY MOTHER'S CORNBREAD DRESSING

1. Boil fat hen in salted water and onion until tender; set aside.
2. Cook corn bread (1 egg and 1/2 cup buttermilk added to 1-1/2 cup self-rising corn meal.)
3. Crumble corn bread in large container, such as a roasting pan. Add four slices of white bread, coarsely torn.
4. Add enough chicken broth to make mixture soft.
5. Add finely-chopped onion to mixture.
6. Add five hard-boiled eggs, chopped.
7. Add 3 or 4 tablespoons of mayonnaise for added richness.
8. If mixture is still dry, add more broth; mixture must be soft.
9. Place fat hen on top and bake about one hour at 375 degrees.

COLLARD GREENS AND 'POT LIKKER'

4 lbs. collard greens, stems removed
Salt and pepper to taste
1/4 lb. fat back (salt pork) or ham hock

Wash the greens in cool water several times to remove grit from field. Place into a large pot of boiling water and boil for about two minutes. Drain the greens, then discard the water. Fill the pot again with enough water to cover greens, bring water to boil, then add greens and fat-back. Bring to a boil; cover and boil slowly for two hours, or until tender. Taste, add salt and pepper as needed. Serve with corn bread, for greens and pot likker.

Note: Collards are best after the frost and cold have made them tender.

CITIFIED COLLARD GREENS

About 4 lbs. fresh collards
1 small onion, minced
1/2 cup water
1/2 cup dry white wine
2 teasp. sugar
1 tabsp. bacon drippings
1/2 cup diced red bell pepper

Remove stems, and wash collards thoroughly several times. Cut into strips (about one inch) and set aside. In a large black pot or Dutch oven, combine onion, water, wine, sugar, and bacon drippings. Bring to a boil. Add collards and red pepper; cover, and cook over medium heat, adding water as needed, for 45 minutes to one hour, or until greens are tender. Serves about 6.

CRACKLIN' BREAD

2 cups sifted corn meal
1 cup cracklings
1 teasp. salt
Water to mix

Break the cracklings into small pieces and pour over them one half cup hot water. Pour into meal, adding enough cold water to mix into a dough. Add salt. Let stand five minutes and if too stiff add a little more water. Shape into small loaves, place on hot pan, in hot oven until slightly brown on top. Reduce heat to medium; bake from 30 to 45 minutes, according to size of pone.

FRIED GREEN TOMATOES

4 green tomatoes
Flour
Salt to taste
Pepper to taste
Oil

Wash tomatoes; cut in 1/2 inch slices. Roll in mixture of salt, pepper, and flour. Fry slowly in oil until browned. Serves 4 to 6.

GOAT CHEESE FRITTERS

1 cup grits
1 tabsp. butter
1/2 cup milk, heated to boiling
2 egg yolks
2 oz. goat cheese
1/8 cup honey
1 tabsp. dry mustard
Salt to taste
Flour (for dredging)
1 egg, beaten
Breadcrumbs
Butter (for frying)

Combine grits, salt, and butter. Add boiling milk; add egg yolks, goat cheese, honey, mustard, and salt to taste. Stir well. Roll mixture in parchment paper to two-inch thick roll. Chill. Cut into medallions and dip into flour, egg wash, then breadcrumbs. Pan fry in butter. Serves 4 to 6.

FRIED OKRA

Cut stem ends off young okra. Cut in 1/4 inch slices. Roll in corn meal, seasoned with salt and pepper. Fry in small amount of oil until brown. Serve hot.

CREAMED CORN

Cut corn from the cob (use sharp knife) and season with salt and pepper to taste. Moisten with milk or cream. Cook in melted butter about 15 minutes on low heat, stirring occasionally.

HAM AND RED-EYE GRAVY

Place several slices of smoked ham in pre-heated cast iron skillet. Brown ham on both sides, then reduce heat and fry slowly until ham sticks to the bottom. Remove ham from skillet and when skillet is hot, add a cup of water. With a metal spatula or egg turner, scrape up the bits of ham stuck to bottom. Stir, simmer for a few minutes, then serve with ham, grits, eggs, and biscuit.

BROWNED BISCUIT

Heat syrup and butter in skillet. Drop in biscuits split in half. Brown on both sides and serve hot with coffee. This is a nice Sunday supper dish.

GRITS AND GREENS

1 cup whipping cream
4 cups chicken broth, divided
1 cup stone-ground grits*
1/4 to 1/2 cup milk
1 pound fresh collard greens**
1/4 cup butter or margarine
1 to 1-1/2 cups freshly grated Parmesan cheese
1/4 to 1/2 teasp. ground pepper
Cooked bacon or ham as garnish

Combine whipping cream and three cups chicken broth in saucepan. Bring to a boil; gradually stir in grits. Cook over medium heat until mixture returns to a boil. Cover, reduce heat, and simmer 25 to 30 minutes, stirring frequently. Gradually add milk, if necessary, for desired consistency.

Remove and discard collard stems and any bad (discolored) spots. Wash greens thoroughly several times. Drain, then cut into 1/2-inch strips. Combine greens and remaining one cup broth in a large skillet; bring to a boil. Cover, reduce heat, and simmer five minutes or until greens are tender. Run cold water over to stop cooking process; drain in colander and then on paper towels.

Add butter, cheese, and pepper to grits, stirring until butter and cheese melt. Stir in drained greens. Cook, stirring constantly, until thoroughly heated. Garnish with ham chunks or crumbled bacon. Serves 6 to 8.

* Can use regular grits if stone-ground grits are not available.

** Raw collards will yield approximately one-fourth the original amount when cooked. Collards are better after they've been through a frost.

CANDIED SWEET POTATOES

4 sweet potatoes
1 cup sugar
1/2 cup water
2 tabsp. butter

Peel and slice potatoes lengthwise, about 1/3 inch thick. Layer potatoes in a baking dish; dot with butter and sprinkle with the cup of sugar, or less sugar according to taste. Add boiling water and bake at 350 degrees, uncovered, for about one hour, or until potatoes are done and syrup is thick.

EMMALINE'S OKRA AND TOMATO PILAU

3 slices bacon, chopped
1 onion
2 cups stewed tomatoes
2 cups thinly sliced okra
Water for rice
2 cups rice
Salt and pepper to taste
Red pepper to taste

Cook chopped bacon in large pan til brown; remove. Fry onion in bacon fat until clear. Add tomatoes and okra and cook until tender, stirring as needed. Add seasonings. Cook rice according to package directions. After rice is done, drain and mix with tomato mixture. Steam, in top of double boiler for 15 to 20 minutes. Add bacon before serving. Serves 8.

HOPPIN' JOHN

2-1/2 cups dry blackeyed peas
8 cups ham stock
Dash Tabasco
1/4 lb. tender collard greens
2 strips bacon, diced
1/2 cup white onion, diced
2-1/2 cups cooked white rice
Salt and pepper to taste

Rinse blackeyed peas in cold water. Place peas and 6 cups of ham stock in large saucepan. Bring to boil, then simmer until tender, but not mushy. Bring remaining two cups of ham stock to boil; add washed, stemmed collards and dash of Tabasco. Simmer until tender, adding water if needed. Strain, cool, then dice collards. Saute bacon until done; add onions, cook until tender. Add diced collards, toss, then mix with warm rice and blackeyed peas. Season to taste. Serves 8.

RINCTUM DIDDIE

1 large onion, chopped
1 tabsp. butter
1 can tomato soup
Salt, pepper, dash Worcestershire
1 lb. rich cheese (sharp Cheddar)
2 eggs, beaten

Cook the onions in butter; add the soup and seasonings, and when hot, add the cheese. Just before serving, add eggs, then pour the mixture over toast.

OLD SOUTHERN BAKED OYSTERS

2 quarts oysters, drained
1/4 cup chopped parsley
1/2 cup green onions
Salt, pepper, Tabasco to taste
1 teasp. Worcestershire
2 tabsp. lemon juice
1/2 cup melted butter
2 cups cracker crumbs
Paprika to taste
3/4 cup milk

Place a layer of oysters in bottom of greased baking dish. Sprinkle with 1/2 of parsley, onions, and seasonings, lemon juice, butter and crumbs. Make another layer of the same and sprinkle with paprika. Just before baking, carefully pour milk into evenly spaced holes. Bake at 375 degrees for 30 minutes, or until firm. Yield: 12 portions.

CAMPHOUSE CHICKEN SUPREME

1 chicken, cut up
1 large onion
4 ribs celery
2 cloves garlic
1/2 bell pepper

Cook chicken and other ingredients together. When chicken is almost done, add two cups rice, cover, and cook slowly until rice is done.

CHICKEN BRUNSWICK STEW

1 chicken
1 quart corn
1 quart tomatoes
1 pint okra
1 pint butterbeans
2 onions
Salt and pepper to taste

Boil chicken until very tender. Pull meat from bones and cut into large cubes. Return to water in which it was cooked. Add vegetables (finely chopped) and cook down until mixture is thick. Cook slowly and stir often to keep from scorching. If necessary to thicken, add bread crumbs in small portions.

FLOSSIE'S OKRA/TOMATO GUMBO

Slice 1/2 pound or so of okra, peel 4 or 5 tomatoes (may use canned); cut one onion and 1/2 bell pepper. Place all ingredients in skillet with a tablespoon or so of bacon drippings; add a little water, salt, and pepper to taste, plus a dash of garlic powder and Worcestershire sauce. Cook covered until tender.

FRIED EGGPLANT

1 cup flour
1 cup bread crumbs
2 eggs
Parseman cheese
1 eggplant, peeled and sliced lengthwise
2 tabsp. olive oil

Place flour and bread crumbs in separate dishes. Lightly beat eggs in a bowl large enough to hold eggplant slices. Dredge eggplant in flour, then dip in egg and then breadcrumbs. Fry in olive oil until golden brown. Sprinkle with Parmesan cheese and ground black pepper to taste. Serves 4.

DEVILED EGGS

A deviled egg plate is a must for Southern occasions. If a bride doesn't get one as a shower gift, her mother buys it for her, for what would picnics, family reunions, or church suppers be without at least two or three plates of deviled eggs?

6 eggs, hard-boiled
1 or 2 tabsp. mayonnaise
1/2 teasp. dry or prepared mustard
2 tabsp. sweet pickle relish
1/4 teasp. salt
Pepper to taste

Cut the eggs in half lengthwise; remove the yolks. Mash yolks with remaining ingredients, then fill the egg whites with the mixture. Sprinkle with paprika.

PERFECT PIMENTO CHEESE

Mix 8 ounces of grated cheddar cheese and 3 ounces of cream cheese. Add a jar of diced pimento and stir in mayonnaise to desired consistency. Add Worcestershire sauce, onion powder, and garlic powder to taste. A pinch of sugar may be added. Use as a sandwich filler or serve with Ritz crackers as an appetizer.

- From the *Mississippi Official and Statictical Register, 1996 - 2000* -

MARLENE'S BREAKFAST MUFFINS

2 cups Bisquick
4 tabsp. sugar
1 egg
1 cup milk (to make batter)

Pour into greased muffin tins. Bake at 350 degrees until done, or until lightly brown on top. When done, cut top and butter.

LOST BREAD

1 cup evaoporated milk
6 eggs
1 tabsp. sugar
1/2 teasp. allspice
1 loaf stale bread

Beat eggs. Add milk and sugar and allspice. Use butter to grease skillet. Dip bread slices in egg mixture and fry on greased skillet until each side is golden brown. Sprinkle with sugar or syrup. Great with coffee or milk!

SALLY LUNN

2 eggs
3/4 cup milk
2 tabsp. sugar
4 teasp. baking powder
1 teasp. salt
2-1/2 cups flour
3 tabsp. butter

Beat eggs together until very light; add milk, sugar and mix as you would a cake, having baking powder and salt sifted with the flour and adding melted butter last. Drop in hot, greased muffin tins, or bake in round layer pans. Bake in 350 degree oven about 30 - 40 minutes, depending upon the depth of the pan. It should be well-cooked, with a thick crust. Cut in pie-shape sections, serve hot, with butter.

FIG-STRAWBERRY PRESERVES

3 cups mashed figs (about 20 med.)
3 cups sugar
1 (6 oz.) pkg. strawberry gelatin
Parafin

Thoroughly mix figs, gelatin, and sugar in a large saucepan. Bring to a boil over medium heat and boil 3 minutes, stirring occasionally. Pour quickly into jars. Cover at once with 1/8-inch hot prrafin. Makes six medium jars.

BERRY BUTTER

1/2 cup butter
1/2 cup blueberry preserves
1/2 cup fresh blueberries
1 tabsp. fresh lemon rind

Cream butter until light and fluffy. Add preserves; mix well. Fold in blueberries, lemon juice and rind. Keep at room temperature until needed.

FIG CHARLOTTE

1 tabsp. gelatin, plain
1 cup sugar
1 pint whipping cream
1/2 teasp. vanilla
1/2 lb. figs, cut fine

Soak the gelatin in 1/4 cup of cold water, then add 1/4 cup of boiling water and the sugar. Whip the cream and add it, with the figs, to the gelatin. Place in a mold or cups to harden.

CLARET SAUCE

1 cup sugar
1 cup water
5 tabsp. claret

Boil the sugar and water for 10 minutes; cool, then add the claret. Serve over vanilla ice cream.

SYLLABUB

- Old recipe -

1 quart cream, 24 hours old
1 cup whole milk
1/2 cup grape juice or orange juice
1 teasp. vanilla
1 cup sugar

Have all ingredients cold; place in a large bowl. With a syllabub churn or egg beater, froth the cream, then fill goblets. The cream and milk will blend so that the mixture won't be too rich. This must be prepared close to serving time else it will fall. If you prefer, 1/4 cup sherry jell maybe used for additional flavoring.

SYLLABUB TODAY

2 pints whipping cream
1 cup Half and Half
1 cup sugar
2/3 cups bourbon

Mix whipping cream, Half and Half, and sugar; stir until sugar is dissolved. Add bourbon and stir. Churn mixture with syllabub churn and skim off froth. Serve froth in glasses or cups. Serves 12 to 14.

PRALINE SAUCE

2 cups dark cane syrup
1/3 cup boiling water
1/3 cup brown sugar
1 cup chopped pecans

Combine all ingredients in saucepan and bring to boil over medium heat. When mixture begins to boil, remove immediately. Cool and store in a covered jar until needed. Serve over vanilla ice cream. Garnish with whipped cream and a cherry, if desired.

WHISKEY BALLS

2 lbs. vanilla wafers
1-1/2 cups crushed pecans
1 cup powdered sugar
1/2 cup white Karo syrup
3/4 cup whiskey

Crush wafers until finely crumbled. Mix with sugar and Karo; add whiskey and pecans. Roll into balls, then roll balls in sifted powdered sugar. Makes about 4 dozen balls.

OLD-FASHIONED PEACH CAKE

(Updated to today's kitchen)

1 pkg. yellow cake mix
1 can (1 lb., 5 oz.) peach pie filling
3 eggs
1/2 teasp. lemon extract
1/2 teasp. chopped nuts

Topping Ingredients:

1/2 cup sugar
1/2 cup flour
1/4 cup butter, softened
1/2 teasp. lemon extract

Cake: Pre-heat oven to 350 degrees. In large bowl, combine dry cake mix, pie filling, eggs, 1/2 teasp. extract, and nuts. Blend at low speed until completely moistened, about one minute. Beat two minutes at medium speed. Spread batter in a greased and floured 13 x 9 x 2 inch pan.

Topping: In a medium bowl, combine with a fork or pastry blender the sugar, flour, softened butter, and 1/2 teasp. extract. Mixture will be crumbly. Sprinkle evenly over batter. Bake at 350 degrees for 40 - 45 minutes until center springs back when touched lightly.

BOURBON PECAN PIE

5 eggs
1 cup brown sugar, packed
1/4 teasp. salt
1/2 cup corn syrup
3 tabsp. butter, melted and cooled
3 tabsp. bourbon
1/2 teasp. vanilla extract
2-1/2 cups pecans, chopped
Unbaked pastry shell

Beat eggs in mixing bowl. Blend in sugar, salt, and corn syrup. Stir in butter, bourbon, and vanilla until blended. Add chopped pecans. Pour mixture into pie shell; place in pre-heated 325 degree oven. Bake until filling is set, about 25 to 30 minutes. Makes one (8-inch) pie.

BANANA PUDDIN'

2 doz. vanilla wafers
6 bananas
1 pint milk
3 eggs
1/2 cup sugar
1 teasp. vanilla
Pinch of salt

First make a boiled custard of the milk, sugar, and yolks of eggs. Add vanilla and salt. Place a layer of wafers then a layer of sliced bananas. Over this, put a portion of the custard. Repeat procedure until all is used, usually three layers, ending with bananas and sauce on top. Make meringue of the three egg whites, using three extra tablespoons of sugar; put on top and bake in 350 degree oven until brown, about ten minutes. Serve hot or cold.

BUTTERMILK PIES

3 cups sugar
6 tabsp. flour
1-1/2 cups buttermilk
5 eggs, beaten
1 cup butter, melted
2 teasp. vanilla extract
2 deep-dish pie crusts, unbaked

Mix sugar, flour, and half of the buttermilk. Add eggs, mix well. Add remaining buttermilk, fold in melted butter; add vanilla. Pour into pie crusts, then bake in 425 degree oven for about ten minutes. Lower oven temperature to 350 degrees and continue baking until knife inserted in center comes out clean, about 30 minutes. Makes two pies.

AUNT AMELIA'S EGGNOG

3/4 cup sugar
10 eggs, separated
1 pint bourbon
1 quart heavy cream

Cream sugar and egg yolks thoroughly. Add whiskey slowly, while stirring constantly, then add the unwhipped cream and finally the stiffly beaten egg whites. Serves 20 - 25.

MISSISSIPPI MINT JULEP

Water
1 teasp. sugar
2 or 3 sprigs mint
Cracked ice
2 jiggers (3 oz.) bourbon
Mint to garnish

Use enough water to dissolve sugar thoroughly. Add two or three sprigs of fresh mint, not bruised. Fill metal cup with finely cracked ice, then add bourbon and stir gently. Add a bit more ice, then allow to stand until frosting occurs. Garnish with mint leaf.

MISS GEORGIA'S RECIPE FOR SHERRY WINE

(Makes one gallon)

Into a stone crock put two pounds seeded raisins, two pounds sugar, one pound raw rice. Dissolve one Fleishman's yeast cake in four quarts luke-warm water. Mix all ingredients thoroughly. Cover crock with cloth and then with lid.

Let stand ten days, stirring thoroughly once each day. Strain, by squeezing through cheese cloth, let stand until the next day (allow 24 hours to settle). Then filter into bottles (buy filter paper from drug store). Put corks in lightly. To insure no bugs, set crock on newspaper and surround with insect powder.

(Miss Georgia's schedule for sherry making: Begin Octob[redacted]
October 29th. Filter into bottles October 30.)

YA'LL COME!

COMMENTS

What you think is important to us. Please send your comments to the address below:

General comment:

____

____

____

The place in Mississippi I'd like to see included:

____

____

- -

ORDER FORM

Please send me ______ copy/copies at $19.95 each, plus $3 shipping and handling.

My name (please print):______________________________________

My address:____

____

My total number of books:______________ Total amount enclosed:___________

Send personal check, money order or credit card (MC/V).

Card Number: ________________________________ Expiration Date: _______

Send comment card or order form to:

[redacted]

PARLANCE PUBLISHING

PO Box 841

[redacted]mbus, Mississippi 39703

[redacted] Thank you -